You'll Be Swell

What to Expect When You Expect That Your Child Will Be A Star

Words & Lyrics by
Allyson Ochs Primac
AKA Momontour

(Alternate title: Everything you ever wanted to know about childhood acting today but had no one to ask because the other parents were too competitive.)

or

What your best, most brutally honest best friend would tell you about the world of childhood acting.

(SPECIAL THANKS TO
GYPSY ROSE LEE FOR THE TITLE)

Dedications

This book would not exist if it were not for my son, Sam, who has allowed me to be a very verbal observant into his world. Thank you Sam, for introducing me to this wonderful, crazy, wacky adventure called acting. I secretly wish that I could have been good at it, and I'm so jealous that you actually are. Thank you for letting me tag along.

Of course, Sam would not be here without my wonderful husband, Craig, who has embraced his son's passion for acting and is a constant support for him. Thank you for being such a great dad to Sam. We are incredibly grateful for your belief in both of us. Thank you for helping create a home for our kids where no dream is too big and no star is out of reach.

Lauren & Aidan: You are both incredible people and I love being your mom. I know that your big brother's after-school activity takes me away from you more than I would like, but you never complain because you are both his biggest fans. I love that you have interests that amaze you just as much as Sam does, and that you understand and support him pursuing his dream. Thank you for being such wonderful kids.

Thank you to all of our family and friends who continually support us by helping out in any way you can. If it takes a village to raise a child, it takes a country to raise a child actor and his siblings. None of this would be possible without all of the people in our lives.

Thank you to all of the young actors and actresses who have let me into their lives and teach me every day about what it means to be brave. Your tenacity and continued belief in yourself despite daily disappointment is awe-inspiring. Every day when I question whether or not I can pursue a dream, all I do is think of all of you and it gives me the courage to go on.

Finally, I would like to dedicate this book to my good friend, Audrey Johnson, the ultimate stage mom in the best way possible. Audrey taught me that the best part of seeing your child onstage is not watching your child become a star. It's watching your child gain self-confidence that will last them a lifetime. We miss you every day and can still hear your laughter and applause at every show, even if you are not here with us anymore.

Chapter Index

Introduction

Chapter One: Parents

Chapter Two: Kids

Chapter Three: Training

Chapter Four: Head shots

Chapter Five: Resume

Chapter Six: The Agent

Chapter Seven: Work Permits

Chapter Eight: Equity vs. Non-Equity for Kids

Chapter Nine: Tours

Chapter Ten: Education

Chapter Eleven: Finances

Chapter Twelve: Pre-teen Years

Chapter Thirteen: College

Conclusion

Introduction

Trust me when I say that I'm the last person who would have ever thought I'd be writing a book like this. I grew up in suburban Detroit and I am licensed to practice law in Michigan and Arizona. I practiced criminal law in Arizona for 15 years. I cannot sing or act. I took jazz dancing growing up and was usually put in the back corner for every recital. I was always given the crappiest parts in school plays. I married a nice Jewish doctor and we have 3 children: Sam, Lauren and Aidan. My life's plan was to pretty much settle into obscurity.

When I found out I was pregnant with Sam, I was so excited. I had no brothers growing up, and I was ready for a life of soccer and baseball. We hired a muralist to paint a baseball field on his bedroom walls and my baby shower was all sports-themed. After Sam was born, I bought him trains and dinosaurs to play with. I took him to soccer class. But all he wanted do was to play with puppets. He hated toy trains and cars and would dance in the back corner of the soccer field. His first words were "I hate my baseball room." We took him to a local theatre production of "Aladdin" when he was 3 and he turned to us and said "'That's what I want to do."

I took him to an audition for a community theatre production at age four. The audition consisted of two hours of dancing and singing. While the other moms sat in the lobby and paced nervously, I sat and read a book and thought how wacky a lot of the moms seemed. When he walked out of the audition, he emerged with a smile on his face that I had never seen before. It was pure joy.

By the age of seven, Sam had been in numerous stage productions around Arizona. There are many wonderful community theaters here and he had lots of great places to choose from. Around that same time, he started taking voice lessons. I was worried because he had been given a singing part in a production of "Annie" and I had never heard him sing. I didn't want him to be too sad when he realized he had been given my horrible singing genes. I wanted a voice teacher to teach him how to best deal with his inherited chalkboard-scratching singing voice and not be embarrassed.

At the end of his first voice lesson, the teacher, a former Broadway actress and singer who had been in everything from the original

4

Broadway production of "Les Mis" to the touring production of "Joseph & The Amazing Technicolor Dreamcoat" came out of the room with a look of shock. I immediately apologized and told her to just do what she could for him to make it through the show. She shook her head and said "No, he can really sing." I told her that lying is not nice and she forced me to listen to him sing. I was stunned. He was great.

By the end of that year, he was doing professional theatre all over Arizona, and by age ten, he landed the role of Pugsley Addams in the National Tour of "The Addams Family." Sam had no agent, and he got the part completely on his own (more on that below.) I had to figure out all of the details and what was expected on my own.

I started a blog called www.momontour.com to document my journey and to help me cope. What I found is that people were fascinated by many things, but mostly they wanted to know about what life was like on the road. I am currently writing a book about all of my crazy adventures as a 40 year old Jewish mom on the road for six months, and I'm hoping you will all get to read it. I had a lot of fun, did a lot of things that I can't believe I did, and learned more about myself and my family that I ever thought I would. It was wild.

Since we have been home from the tour, Sam has gotten taller and his voice is changing and getting deeper every day and we are exploring the worlds of television, film, and commercials. Our location in Arizona makes it easy for us to go back and forth to Los Angeles if needed.

In the meanwhile, a lot of people have contacted me with questions about how to get their children involved in show business. While I consider myself the anti-stage mom, mostly because I am still stunned that I have a child that has actual talent (and even that embarrasses me to say). However, what I realized is that when Sam got the offer to be in the Tour, I had so many of these similar questions and I didn't have anyone to ask. I looked for books about what it would be like on tour, or what types of things I should expect. Nothing existed.

Through theatre friends, I was given phone numbers of moms throughout the country who had been on tour with their children. When I would call these women, they were guarded in their answers and sometimes downright rude. I do realize there are only a few parts out there for kids, but my feeling is that we are all in this together. I promised myself that I would always be helpful to other parents seeking information, because it really is such an unusual and confusing world.

So, I have put together this e-book to help answer the majority of questions I receive about childhood show business. I hope that this helps you figure out A) if you want to do this with your child and B) how to navigate it if you do.

Enjoy!

Allyson Primack
Lawyer, Mom, Philanthropist, Writer and Anti-Stage Mom.

CHAPTER ONE:

PARENTS

If you are a mom, you have already figured out by now that there are several different types of parents out there. When you are in parent-toddler classes, there are the mothers who brag that their children are crawling, while yours is just sitting around playing with their toes. As they start talking, there are the moms on the playground who insist that their child can recite the Declaration of Independence at age one, while yours is excited to say "ball." It goes on and on as the kids get older.

In the acting world, it is just like that. But worse. You may not believe me, but it's true. Now, I know that the world in 2014 is not what it was when I was growing up in the 1970s. You cannot just take dance class anymore. You must be on a competitive dance team. Gymnastics is not just tumbling on mats. It is a full-time job. Soccer, hockey, and baseball teams don't travel to a different city to compete anymore: they travel around the country. And while I know that all activities today seem to require Olympic-style training and lifestyles, there is still something a little different to me about this acting thing.

What I see in the acting world is more disturbing to me because I see parents who are trying to fulfill their own life dreams through their children. And while yes, I know that cheerleading moms do the same thing, what disturbs me about this is that a majority of the acting world is less about talent and ability, and more about having a certain look or a sound. I have seen dozens of talented kids get passed over for the ones who "look the part." If you, as a parent, cannot relay that to your child, to keep them grounded and to remind them that this is not their only option in life, it can be devastating. And the devastation is not limited to the child. It is often the parent who cannot deal with their child's rejection.

I have seen mothers who slap their children in the audition room when they say they are tired of waiting around (Rule #1: Acting requires A LOT of waiting around.) I have seen mothers who feed their children unhealthy food so that they are marketable to play "the fat kid." I spoke to a mother of an 11 year old girl, who, after many rejections, was going to take her to a plastic surgeon to get her "big ears fixed."

I want to clarify that I am not singling out mothers in this Chapter. I have seen many, many stage fathers out there. There are lots of dads that leave their positions as the full-time breadwinner to shuttle their child to auditions. I have known several fathers who have adjusted their career or work schedule to be able to be away with their child actor at a moment's notice. The term "stage mom" is not exclusive to one gender over another.

That being said, if you are going to go into this with the knowledge that the entire business is a bit of a crap shoot, I can give you some additional advice.

A. Marital Status: If you are married, you need to make sure that your spouse understands what all of this involves. You need to be on the same team as to what you will or will not do for your child. If you agree in advance that you will relocate for a job for your child, it will cut down on hours of family drama. Often, the out of state jobs are for short periods of time (ie a movie shoot), or longer (for a touring show), and you need to decide how you would do that as a family. You also need to discuss how much money you are willing to spend to make this dream of your child's come true. As you will read below, acting is a costly profession, and discussing finances in advance will lessen the fights you will have when the bills come in. Finally, I do suggest that your marriage is on steady ground to begin with before proceeding in this career. You will be apart for a lot of the time, especially if your child does book a job far away. If you or your spouse cannot handle that, I would suggest you wait until your child is 18.

B. Siblings: As I said, I have two children younger than Sam. My daughter Lauren is very involved in after-school activities, and my son Aidan has some educational & behavioral needs that require an all-hands-on deck approach. If you do not have a good support system at home, please pause before you continue with this world for your acting child. You need family members, friends, trustworthy teachers and babysitters, to keep the world stable for your other children. There is no way to stop them being resentful of their sibling or jealous of the time they spend with you, but there are ways to make sure they feel just as special and unique. I can guarantee years of anger and problems to come on behalf of your child's siblings if you do not.

I often say that this acting thing is really perfect for a single parent with one child, or a person in a miserable marriage with one child. Having other children who have lives of their own makes a life of being able to pick up and go at a moment's notice extremely difficult. The best case scenario that I have seen is when your child actor is the youngest child in the family, and the older siblings have gone off to college. Other great attributes for this lifestyle in which there are other children involved are private jets and live-in nannies and drivers. (I will admit up front that we hired a live-in au pair for the time period that Sam was on tour. She was a gorgeous, brilliant teenager from Austria, and if you think I'm crazy for leaving her with my family, you are not alone! My Momontour book will let you know how crazy it all was...)

Another note: some parents choose to make this situation easier by forcing ALL of their children to be involved in acting. Sometimes this is helpful and sometimes this just makes it worse. If the siblings have other interests, being pushed to do what their big brother does just to "make it easier on mom," is just creating more problems. It's fine if they have the same passion as their sibling, and will be able to handle it if their sibling continues to shine and they do not have the same amount of success. If this is not the case, I would ask you to re-evaluate that idea.

C. Behavior of Parent

Most casting directors agree, that like it or not, when you hire the kid, you hire the parent. If the parent is rude or obnoxious, they will unfortunately cause problems for the child. I will say this many times in this book, but the acting world is very small. Think of your hometown. If someone has a bad reputation, word gets around fast. Let me tell you, the acting world is just as small. There are children who will not be cast simply because the producers do not want their parents on-set. Below are some tips on how to behave so that you are being the best parent you can be for your child.

1. **Get off your high horse:** To begin with, get rid of any notions that you or your child are any more special than any other person in the audition room. No one wants to sit around and wait, and everyone wants their child to be alert and at their best for the audition. Many kids will come into auditions with an appointment time, but often will arrive to find out that several children are booked at that exact same time. Do not make a scene or demand to be seen first. The best advice I can tell you is to always arrive early. If it is an open call, arrive at least a half hour before the doors open. If you have an appointment, the advice is the same. You do not want you or your child to arrive stressed out from running late. This will calm all nerves and attitudes.

Be as polite and respectful to everyone in that room as you would be at a job interview of your own. It is, in a way, an interview/audition for you as well.

2. Do Not Bribe Anyone. This sounds like a preposterous thing to say, but let me tell you, it is coming from a place of knowledge. I have seen parents offer directors all sorts of things to get their children cast in shows. In smaller, local venues, this can work for a short period of time, especially when those theatres need the money or the connections that you offer to them. But if your child's talent does not match the donations, it puts your child in a terrible position. It will ruin their reputation as an actor, and the community will question every role they are offered in the future. Further, this does not work on Broadway, so you are giving them a false sense of what their future holds. Let them figure out who they are and who they are not at an early age so that they are realistic about what they can achieve on their own.

3. Be Smart: Once your child books a role, if you do not have an agent or a manager (more about that below), you need an entertainment attorney to go over contracts and documents. Before you hire an agent, check out their background and references. There are several websites and books that can tell you if your potential agent is legitimate. There are many people in this business who can take advantage of a parent's desperation to get their child a job, so make sure you are doing all you can to advocate for your child.

Also, make sure you protect yourself and your own interests. If you are signing documents agreeing to the responsibilities of being an on-set guardian, make sure that these documents, too, are reviewed by an attorney.

4. Social Media: Although we aren't as tech savvy as our kids, most of us adults do use some form of social media. Whether it be Facebook, Twitter or Instagram (anything more than this I simply don't know how to use), we use it for a variety of reasons. As parents, we can talk about the joys and frustrations that our children provide for us on a daily basis (case in point: the "Momontour" blog that once the tour itself ended, has now become a vehicle for me to chat about my own observations as a parent.) It is perfectly common and acceptable to brag about your child's success, and to sometimes lament how the world can be unfair. This is especially true of parents involved in the acting

11

community when it comes to casting of shows and the success of others who don't seem to be deserving of all their success.

Please remember that casting directors, producers, agents, and other actors use these social media tools as well. Being that it's a small world in the acting community, chances are your words will be spread to lots and lots of people. Be mindful that you do not want to put anything out there on social media that you would hurt your child's career.

Conclusion

Before I end this chapter, I just want to say that some of my closest friends are fellow stage parents. There are wonderful people out there who are giving it their all because their child loves to be on stage. I have met parents who are heartbroken that they cannot afford to send their children to the best acting classes, workshops and camps. I have seen parents crushed due to their child's heartbreak at not getting that dream role. But what I love about these parents is that they are doing it all for their child. Their expectations are realistic and they would never stab another parent in the back for the sake of their child's career.

That is what I want you to ask yourself every few months: "Am I doing this for myself or for my child? If my child told me tomorrow that they want to focus on lacrosse instead of acting, will I be more disappointed than I should be?" You need to keep yourself in check and focused as much as your child. It is easy to get caught up in the fun and glamour of being the parent of a star. It is an incredible feeling. But remember you are also the parent of a child who is still growing and changing. You need to be able to let it go if they want to.

CHAPTER TWO: KIDS

Every single child dreams of being famous. Admit it, even you thought about it when you were growing up. You pictured your name in lights, getting tons of attention and adoration from fans. You dreamed of seeing yourself in magazines and on television shows. Hours of your childhood were spent daydreaming about a world in which limos and private planes took you wherever you wanted to go. Perhaps you still think about it today. And now that the reality of your own life has set it, you have begun dreaming of this future for your child.

Let me begin by saying that it takes a certain type of child to be able to be successful in the acting world. Even the most talented, outgoing child will not make it as an actor if they do not have the right tools. These tools cannot be purchased at a store or taught in a class. It is just part of the genetic make-up of the child.

A. The Five "Ps":

I have created what I call the 5 "P"s for child actors. In order to really succeed, your child must genuinely have all 5 "P"s.

1. Passion: As with any activity that can overtake your life, you must have an overwhelming passion for what you do. Tennis and golf players are constantly thinking about their strokes. Teachers are always thinking how to turn a simple activity into a learning lesson. Actors are no different. If you want to make acting your career, you must love it. An actor must love the craft of acting as much as being onstage. They must want to learn and perfect their craft every single day.

I use Sam as an example simply because I live with him and have known him his whole life. Sam loves acting. And what I mean by that is that he doesn't just love to act. He loves to watch other actors. He loves to talk to other actors about acting. He is constantly researching the latest Tony nominated shows and actors: how they got their start and where they trained. He watches "the making of" videos on Youtube to study how special effects were created and what the actor had to do to be part of the process. His favorite place to be is in rehearsal for a show. He is unhappy and unsettled if he is not rehearsing for something. He never asks for "a break."

It is for this reason that I do not worry about him as a child actor. He absolutely lives for acting and his passion startles many people who meet him. I do think it is unusual for a person to know exactly what they want from the moment they are born. Many of us spend our entire lives figuring out what we are passionate about. If you are lucky enough to know very early on, then you should be able to develop that passion as long as you live.

2. Patience: Can your child sit still for long periods of time? Can they lower their voices or turn down their physical energy when asked to? If the answer is no, you may want to wait until they can. Acting is many things: it is fun, exciting, physical and emotional. But the one thing it is not, is structured. Every single day on a set is different. Every single show is different. Even shows that have opened months ago require constant tinkering and changing. Children are asked to sit and be quiet while blocking is changed, choreography is figured out, or a director needs to set up a take. Children often have to sit backstage for hours until they go onstage. Kids need to be able to entertain themselves with books, small electronics, or arts and crafts while waiting these things out. I have seen several children with way too much physical energy cause problems during shows or on sets. These children simply do not have the patience that acting requires.

Not every stage production can be "Oliver!" and not every television show can be "The Brady Bunch." (Sorry for the 70s references, but I can't remember the names of half of the shows on t.v. today!) The point is that your child can very often be the only child in the play or the movie. This can be lonely and isolating, especially if it is for long periods of time. Siblings are often not allowed while your child is working, and the adults they are working with are usually too busy to spend quality time laying with your child. Sam has been in several shows where he is the only child. "The Addams Family" had two young actors to alternate playing Pugsley, but the boys were not together backstage once the show opened. Sam usually had his own dressing room so that he was not put in a position to be in a room full of half-dressed men. This can be lonely, especially in Sam's case where he was on the road for 6 months with this cast.

Childhood is a time to make memories and have fun and play. Acting is hard work. It is a job that requires a serious attitude and commitment.

3. Persistence: One of the worst words in the English language is "rejection." Just the word alone brings back painful feelings. As a child, rejection includes of getting picked for dodgeball during gym class, not getting asked to the school dance by your crush, not getting invited to the cool kid's party, or not getting that summer job you thought you were sure to get. My own memories of childhood rejection are always there with me, especially now that I am a parent and I see my kids going through their own forms of social and emotional rejection. I still get upset thinking about some of the most painful of these rejections.

Unfortunately, acting involves constant rejection. Kids who make acting their hobby growing up know this right away. It is not unlikely for a child to lose out on the starring part in the camp show or the school play and have to continue to smile as they stand in the corner as an ensemble member. (All the while you and your child sit there and think how much better your child would have done in that role.)

This can turn many children off from pursuing acting as a career, and that's a good thing. If you can't handle rejection, acting is not for you. I'm sure there are statistics on this, but I would have to guess that 99 % of professional acting is filled with rejection. Even for the ones who have already "made it."

Kids who attempt to become professional actors at a young age deal with rejection all the time. In order to be able to keep going on as an actor, your child must understand that most of the time, rejection is not personal. It is very much a "try and try and you may succeed" type of business. It is normal to feel sad, frustrated, or angry at a lot of rejection. The key to a successful child actor is the ability to quickly brush aside this rejection and go on to the next audition.

There is no guarantee that this persistence will pay off. There are tons of childhood actors out there who have never gotten a big role. There are kids who spend every single day at an audition for one job or another. No one can ever promise them that one day, something big will happen for them. The sad reality is that there are only a handful of kids who truly succeed early on in their careers. (And then there are even sadder stories about the ones who do get discovered at an early age, only to never land a role again or to be pigeonholed as a child actor. The stories of the drugs and alcohol abuse that comes with such bitter disappointment could fill up a whole book.)

4. Pluckiness: Quick: think of that little kid on t.v. that makes you instantly smile no matter what they are doing. What about Annie singing "Tomorrow" with that gleam in her eye and sparkle in her step makes you believe that it will all turn out fine. Miranda Cosgrove's happy smile and natural comedic skills in shows like "I Carly" makes you cheer her on, even with the silly story lines and canned laughter. Drew Barrymore in "E.T." makes you laugh and cry every single time you watch it.

These kids have something that no one can teach you: they have "it." They have a likability that some directors will call organic. It is not an act, they are just who they are, and they are very appealing. I am not an acting teacher or a director, but I really don't believe this can be taught. No amount of money or training can give a child the likability factor. Think of Quvenzhane Wallis, the little girl from "Beasts of the Southern Wild" and the new "Annie" movie. She was just 5 years old at the time of the "Beasts" audition, and had never acted in her life. She went to an open casting call in her hometown in Louisiana, and had such a natural ability to draw people in that she landed the role that was originally written for an 11 year old. During the initial casting process for "Matilda" on Broadway, the casting directors were insistent on casting kids who were untrained and just seemed "real." I have seen recent audition notices for "Matilda" and this still seems to be what they are looking for in replacement children.

This is not to say that if your child doesn't seem to have what directors are looking for as a child that they will not be able to act professionally as adults. The natural pluckiness that is required of child actors is not essential for older actors.

5. Plausibility: Close your eyes and think of the little boy in "Home Alone." What instantly comes to mind? Those bright blue eyes and adorable face. How about "Webster?" (sorry, another 70s reference.) The beautiful little black boy with the chubby face and short stature. When it comes to kids in t.v. and film, whether or not you want to admit it, there is a look. Kids don't want to watch other children on screen that they would not want to hang out with in real life. It has to be plausible that Adam Sandler would fall in love with a little boy dropped on his doorstep and change his life so that he can have a stable home for him. And in order for it to be plausible, he has to be cute.

The only time you don't have to be absolutely adorable to be onscreen is if you are playing the kid that's "a mess." Audiences love to laugh at the funny-looking or overly chubby kid. But do you really want your child to be cast in a film solely for the fact that they are easily laughed at for their appearance? For many parents, the answer is yes. This is something that you have to decide if you realize that your child is not considered a "classic beauty."

This is the same in theatre. Pugsley has to be somewhat short and stout. Chip in "Beauty and the Beast" has to be a cute little boy that you could picture as a teacup. Young Cosette in Les Miserables has to have an intense face and pure beauty that you could picture as a street urchin and later as a beauty that would cause a revolutionary soldier to fall in love at first sight. As a well-known theatre director says at each and every audition he holds, " Acting is a matching process. You may be a lion. And you may be the best lion in town. But we are casting a mouse. So if you don't get cast in this production, remember that it has nothing to do with how talented you are." It has to be plausible that this actor is playing this role in order for it to capture the audience's attention.

The area that this is most true in is <u>commercials</u>. When kids are cast in commercials, it is usually because they are casting some sort of "family unit" to sell a product. It has to be plausible that your child would be part of that family. Even if your daughter has beautiful blonde hair and piercing green eyes, if she is not Hispanic, she cannot be part of that family unit going to "Peter Piper Pizza" after school. If your son is too tall in relation to the father cast in the print ad, they will go with another boy who is shorter. Out of every form of childhood acting, this is the most frustrating for children. Hundreds of children are seen and casting agents generally only pick the one who best fits the look they need.

B. Behavior: I have a friend whose son was cast in a well-known film. He was young at the time, and not particularly excited about being on a set. However, he looked exactly like the main actor as a young boy, and he was cast straight off of his headshot. He and his mom were flown to an exotic location to shoot one scene. In the scene, he was supposed to eat a cookie and sit on the toilet. He didn't want to do either. So, he kept eating the cookie and not listening to the director. The director yelled at both the child and the mom and told her there was another boy on set who was ready to do this scene. After several takes, the boy did his job and then vomited up the cookies. His scene was cut from the film and his name does not appear in the credits.

18

This a cautionary tale for those of you who are unsure if your child is ready to behave on a set or backstage, rehearsing or filming the same scene over and over, and then sitting quietly for long periods of time. If you do not think your child is able to behave in an appropriate manner while backstage, on a tour bus, or on a set, then please re-consider. The last thing you want to do is to ruin any chances for this child to make it as an actor when they are older.

CHAPTER THREE:
TRAINING

As with any skill, the best thing to do if you want to get better is to practice, practice, practice. I can't think of any sport in the world that does not require some form of training. Acting, dancing, and singing are no different from any of those sports. You must continue to train, even once you are professional.

If your child wants to be a stage actor only, the training is different from that of an on-camera actor. However, I do suggest that every child, at some point, try performing in a play or a musical. For many actors, being on stage on front of a live audience gave them the best training they could ever get to pursue a career on film. Immediate audience feedback tells actors what works and what does not. The earlier you start learning that, the better you will be.

Below are some suggested forms of training for your child. I know that these classes, camps and workshops can be costly for many families, so I hope that your city or town offers a wide variety of options to choose from.

A. Voice Lessons:

If your child wants to be in a musical, or to be the next triple-threat like Justin Timberlake, they are going to have to be able to carry a tune. This is true even if your child dreams of life as a professional dancer. There are more and more "triple threats" out there, and having incredible dancing or acting skills alone is not enough anymore

Most auditions for musical theatre productions require that your child sing 16-32 bars of music. There will almost always be a pianist at the audition, so bringing sheet music is best, although it is also acceptable to bring a CD of the music for them to sing along to. The key to a successful audition is that your child be able to correctly sing the song that they bring. This is where a voice teacher comes in very handy.

There are very few of us who can pick up sheet music to a song and be able start singing it in the correct key. Almost any song can be adjusted to fit a person's range. The important thing is to be able to know what "key" your child can sing in. This is especially true for boys. Sam started out being able to sing very high and was considered a "tenor."

However, within that range, he was trained by his voice teacher which notes (high "C" vs. "D") he could "hit" and which notes were simply too high for his voice. Your voice teacher should be able to correctly figure out which type of singer your child is before his/her audition and which audition songs will showcase their voice the best.

Out of all of the types of training, this is the one that needs the most attention. The reason is simple: your child's voice changes every single day. Unfortunately for them, it gets lower and lower as they grow older (this applies to girls as well.) If your child is cast in a show that will play for long periods of time (ie over a month), it is suggested they see a voice teacher on the side to continue to practice singing their songs. Once your child is cast as "Annie" on Broadway, she still needs to be able to adjust "Maybe" and "Tomorrow" over the run of the show because her voice will change. Even the slightest vocal changes are important to make note of for a singer. The reason for this is something that all singers fear: vocal nodes. If a singer does not receive the proper training, they could develop nodes on their vocal cords that can require surgery and in rare instances can ruin a singer's career. This is especially true of developing boys and girls who are belting out notes day after day that their vocal cords cannot handle. The stress of these high notes contribute to their vocal nodes. Vocal health is key to long-term success.

One thing I have learned as Sam's voice has gone from a tenor to almost a baritone, is that there are often two different types of vocal training needed. A "tween/teen" needs a teacher who is trained in vocal development to make sure that he or she re-learns how to sing in their "new voice." This is highly technical, and often requires completely starting over and learning how to sing again. Sam's vocal coach says it is like getting a brand new instrument to play. You must start with the basics again and learn what your new instrument is capable of doing.

Part of vocal coaching includes knowing how to correctly hold your body while singing. There is actually something called vocal posture. In order to get the most out of your voice as possible, you need to know how to stand and how hold your head, neck and shoulders. This is also true of breathing while singing. Knowing when to take those breaths can make all the difference in the world to a singer trying to master a new song.

Just as important is a voice teacher who can help your child pick out the correct audition song. Often these two teachers can be wrapped up into one person, but we have found that Sam has one voice teacher

22

who is wonderful at prepping him in vocal posture and technique and one who is fantastic at choosing fun, different songs for each audition.

When we are out of town, it is sometimes interesting to try a local voice teacher for one or two lessons, just to pick up new audition songs or techniques.

Here are a few tips I have picked up along the way about choosing audition songs:

1. *Do not sing a song from the show you are auditioning for!!!* This is the cardinal rule of auditioning. Most voice teachers know this, but some do not, so please make sure that your child doesn't walk into an audition for "Annie" singing "Tomorrow." (Unless it is specifically requested in the audition notice.) Usually, the casting director will have your child sing a song or two from the show at a callback.

2. *Do not have your child sing a song that is older than they are.* For example, do not have your child sing "Good Morning, Baltimore" from the teenage show "Hairspray" at an audition if they are 10 years old. Your 12 year old son should not sing a song that Nathan Lane sang from "The Producers." Choose an age-appropriate song, and try to find one that is not unique and overdone. (Note: To find the most popular songs, just google "overdone audition songs" and you will find several no-nos from well-known casting directors.)

3. *No pop music or rock songs if your child is auditioning for a Broadway-style show, unless it is specifically requested by the casting directors* (ie, for the show "Motown," the child auditioning for young Michael Jackson should be prepared to sing an R & B song.) However, if your child is auditioning for a Disney or Nickelodeon television show, and they can also sing, they would rather hear your child sing a Justin Bieber song than a song from Les Miserables.

4. *Every singer should have a "book" of songs that they can bring to auditions.* This book should consist of a variety of music. We usually have in Sam's book one classic, one modern, and one different/unique song at all times. These songs keep changing as his voice gets lower but there will always be a wide variety to choose from in his book. Casting directors will often ask your child to sing more than one song at an initial audition to get a full picture of their vocal abilities.

5. *Practice, practice, practice*: The biggest disaster audition stories usually start with the words, "I didn't memorize the song." Forgetting lyrics, pausing, or starting over is distracting to both the singer and the casting director. Make sure that if your child has chosen a new song that they have memorized the melody and the lyrics. Your child should not need to hold their sheet music as they sing. The director wants to be in the moment with your child and to see their expressions when they sing. If there is a sheet of paper covering his face while singing in front of casting directors, it will not allow for a fully organic audition.

Note on "Sides": Often at an audition, the casting director will have the kids read lines from a scene that is actually in the show. If you are lucky, the casting director will give you the sides in advance of the audition via email. This gives your child time to practice saying these lines with the correct emotion and to learn any sort of required dialect in advance. Sam usually tries to memorize these lines in advance of the audition so that he can be as authentic as he would be onstage. If he is given the sides at the audition, he usually tries as hard as possible to get the general feel of the scene and to figure out how to pronounce any difficult or unusual words before going into the audition room. When he was younger, he would ask me to practice with him. Now, he goes into a quiet place so he can focus.

B. Community Theaters: We come from Arizona, where we are very lucky to have literally dozens of community theaters to choose from. Our theaters range from ones I like to call "pay to play" all the way to professional theatre. I will explain the different types of theaters that we have in our home state. Of course, I don't know if every town will have all of these types of theaters but there should be at least some of them to choose from where you live.

1. School/Church plays: When I was growing up in Michigan, these were the staples of my childhood as far as theatre opportunities. Elementary, middle, and high school plays were, and still are, excellent places to hone your craft. These teachers are some of the most passionate ones out there. They work long hours, painting their own sets and making their own costumes, with very little pay. But they love what they do and many have bachelor's degrees from universities with

24

theatre programs. You will often find that these teachers have also been professional actors at one time in their lives.

I grew up with Elizabeth Berkley, and she did school plays and was very involved in a local dance studio. When she was in high school, she decided she wanted to be a professional actress. Her family made the incredible decision to move from Michigan to Los Angeles to help her with her career. Shortly after that, she was cast on "Saved By The Bell." Being a part of school plays and becoming an expert dancer was enough to get her launched into a sitcom and a career in acting. This is also true for Arizona native Emma Stone, who had only local theatre credits to her name before convincing her parents to allow her to drop out of high school and move with her to Los Angeles to pursue an acting career. She won a role on a reality show about The Partridge Family and has not stopped working since.

2. Pay to Play: (also known as "no cut"): If you want to see if your child could handle the rigors of rehearsing, staging, and performing in a production that will have a longer run than a school play, this a great option. These types of productions can be produced in almost any facility. A YMCA, library, or after-school enrichment program can provide your child with a very good beginning theatrical experience. Every single child who auditions will get cast, and the parents are required to pay some sort of fee to have their child in the show. This can be a one-time fee of $100, or you may be required to pay for costumes. One of our local theatres requires that the parents sell a certain amount of tickets in order for their child to participate.

These shows will often advertise to the general public, so your child will get experience performing in front of a large audience. The shows are often double, triple or quadruple cast so that as many children as possible can get a chance at doing a "lead" role with special lines or dances. There is usually a rotating schedule as to when your child will play their special role and when they do not. This also gives children the opportunity to learn to be part of an ensemble when they are not playing their "leads." These shows can run several weekends so it will teach your child about the consistency and energy you need to be in a show that runs for a long period of time. If their goal is Broadway, your child will be performing the same show, 8 times a week, for months at a time.

What I love the most about this type of theatre is that your child will also learn about the reality of not getting the part that they want. If you stick with the no-cut theatre for a while, there will be some shows where your child lands the part that they want, and sometimes they will not. Sam's second theatre production was "Beauty and the Beast" at age 5, and he got the coveted part of the "Footstool." The next show was "Alice in Wonderland" and he was cast in the ensemble as a "pearl." He was disappointed, but his love of being on stage trumped his sadness, and he went on to do 20 more of these types of shows. Sometimes he was in the ensemble, in a part such as "Royal Trumpeter #4" (Into the Woods), and sometimes he was a special role that had a few lines, such as the Young Kangaroo (Seussical). No matter the role, each show was a great experience and learning opportunity.

3. <u>Semi-professional ("cut" theaters- some or no pay):</u> In Metropolitan Phoenix, we are lucky enough to have theaters that put on professional-quality productions that cast kids up to age 18. These theaters have open casting calls for shows such as "Peter Pan" or "Legally Blonde" with professional sets, costumes, staging and lighting. There will often be over 100 kids who will come to the auditions, but and only a fraction of those who audition will get a part.

If the show they are producing has a large ensemble, it provides for more opportunities. But, if they are doing a show such as "You're A Good Man Charlie Brown," there are only a few characters that are written into the script. The theaters have to pay publishing companies for the rights to these shows, and they cannot edit or alter the scripts to add parts unless noted by the authors. These shows are usually not double-cast, and the kids will rehearse long hours after school and on weekends, and perform for several weekends or months.

We also have community theaters that cast mostly adults. These productions are very well-done, and generally cast actors that have full-time jobs in different fields other than acting. Adult community theatre productions will often need a child or two, or sometimes several, for part of their cast. Shows such as "Fiddler on the Roof", "The Sound of Music" and "Tommy" need young actors to round out their adult cast. These are wonderful experiences for young actors to learn from older, more experienced actors. Keep in mind that because rehearsals are after-work hours, your child will be out late rehearsing, often until 10 p.m. or later during school, so you want to check the rehearsal schedule before having your child audition if this is a concern for you or your child. These productions usually double-cast the child parts so that the children are not overworked.

Community theatre productions are excellent opportunities to expose your kids to local theatre critics and reviewers, who will often come see the shows and publish their reviews in local newspapers and online.

4. <u>Professional theatre (paid theatre)</u>: Professional theatrical productions are produced and performed locally throughout the country, but they are cast with local and out-of-state equity actors. These productions are performed at large, Broadway-quality theaters and the shows can run for up to 2 months. Again, adult shows often need a child or two and will hold open casting calls. These shows are generally double or even triple cast for the younger actors to lessen the amount of hours they will be needed each week. Professional theatrical productions will usually have 8 shows per week, and this can be hard on school-aged children. Often, week-night productions will begin at 7 or 8 p.m. and end well after 10 p.m., and anyone who is a parent knows how hard it is to wake up a child who has been up late. This can also affect your child's performance at school and their behavior at home.

The fantastic bonus of performing in an equity production is that because there is a union involved, there are set, strict hours for rehearsals and productions. If the end of day time for rehearsal is scheduled for 10:00 p.m., your child will be done at 10:00 on the dot and not a moment later. This is not true for most theaters, as most of the theatre world runs on a very loose schedule. I have found that while artists are incredibly creative, generous, and giving, the one thing they are not is punctual.

Equity theatre productions will usually pay your child a small stipend for the work that they do on the show. It is thrilling to see your child's name on a paycheck, and they also learn the value of hard work.

A final word on local theatre productions: rehearsing for a show is all-consuming, and your child will often go straight from school to rehearsal to bed. I recommend putting all other activities on hold while your child is in rehearsals. Extra practices can be added at a moment's notice, and your child will often be asked to arrive earlier or come later than what was on the printed schedule that you receive at the beginning of the rehearsal process. Having the flexibility to say yes, and knowing that your child will have time-off on the days they are not rehearsing, is really the key to the entire process. Once the show opens, feel free to resume the swimming and tennis practices, as long as your child wants to do so. Many may ask to wait until the entire run has ended. The most important thing is to listen to your child and watch for signs of exhaustion.

C. Acting Classes: Even if your city or town does not have a slew of theaters to choose from, they will most likely have an acting studio somewhere nearby. These studios also usually offer voice lessons and classes with instructors who will teach them how to play a variety of musical instruments. Acting classes can come in all different forms: from improv classes to musical theatre to the newest popular class: "Glee."

Acting classes usually focus more on acting games and exercises, which are just as important as practicing lines and being on stage. They teach you how to hold your body while in front of an audience and how to project so that your voice is heard all the way to the back of the stage.

The classes will teach you how to warm yourself up before an audition or show, and how to improvise a situation or an experience. The skill improvisation is a highly under looked talent. There have been many, many auditions that Sam has been on, from stage to screen, where he is asked to improvise. Casting directors want to see what your child will do in a situation that calls for improvisation. Acting classes often conclude with a showcase for families to see what their kids have learned. I highly recommend your child take as many acting classes as they can.

1. *On Camera*: When Sam finished with the tour, we decided to try out the on-camera aspect of acting. Sam had returned from the tour five inches taller, and his voice was several octaves deeper. We realized that he was no longer going to be able to play the little boy in a play, and he wasn't old enough to play a teenage role. He was in the twilight zone of the theatre world, so we decided to check out something different.

Sam had done one local industrial commercial for a door-lock company in Arizona when he was eight years old, in which he was playing baseball with his father. There were no spoken lines and the shoot took about an hour. That was the total extent of his on-camera experience besides some television interviews he gave about theatre. However, as we were submitting him for more and more on-camera auditions, we started noticing the need for a "reel." Sometimes called a "sizzle reel," this is a collection of clips of an actor's on-camera experience. In order to have a reel, your child needs to start having on-camera experience.

a. *On-Camera Classes:* When we met with agents in L.A., they would glance at his resume and read the rave reviews written by newspaper critics about his acting. While they were impressed with his theatrical experience, they they all said the same thing: he needs to take on-camera acting classes. Stage acting is a completely different world from on-camera acting. You need to learn to bring it down several notches, and how to play to the camera instead of a live audience. When we returned from our trip to L.AI, we found that there were several on-camera acting classes offered in Arizona. The on-camera acting studios offer classes that range from "Disney Show Acting" to "Commercial Acting" to "On Camera Audition Techniques." These classes will often conclude with your child performing in a scene or two that will be professional filmed and can be used in their reel.

b. *Student Films:* This is probably the #1 way to add to a reel when you don't have any professional commercial or t.v. clips. Students at film schools all over the country need to write, produce, and direct short films to be used for final exams or for school film festivals. While student films generally do not provide any pay, they do give your child an excellent clip or two to add to their reel. I know adult actors who will do student films to add more dimension to their existing reels (ie they will do a comedic role in a student film if their reel contains only dramatic moments or too many commercials.)

c. *Short Films/Documentaries:* Another excellent way to add to the reel is to do a short film or documentary. Not only are these great tools to stretch your acting muscles, but these films are often shown at film festivals throughout the country, and you never know who may be in attendance. Short films are produced by professional writers, directors and producers, and some will provide some compensation or per diem. Some films even get expanded to be made into longer films or are picked up by larger production companies for distribution.

D. Camps : I grew up going to sleep-away camp for 10 years in northern Michigan. I feel it helped me learn to be independent and to deal with situations on my own, without my parents' help. I really wanted my children to experience the same thing, but with Sam, he made it clear that he didn't want to be in any situation where there he would have to play sports.

So, we launched our search for overnight camps that focused on acting. What we found really made us happy. There are several options to choose from throughout the country; everywhere from California to Michigan to New York. Some of the most well-known camps are located in the Catskill region of New York. French Woods is a camp that includes both performing arts and other fun activities including circus training. Sam immediately focused on one in upstate New York called Stagedoor Manor. He was fascinated by all of the celebrities that attended Stagedoor as kids, and by the fact that the campers dance, sing and act almost 24 hours a day.

There is no audition process for a majority of theatre camps. All that is needed is just an application and patience, along with the financial means to get your child there if there is a spot for him. We sent in our application to Stagedoor the summer that Sam was 9 years old, and he was accepted to attend the following summer. At Stagedoor and several other very popular acting camps, priority is given to previous campers. The remaining spots are given in order that the applications are received by the camp office. There are 3 sessions, and if your schedule allows it, the best advice is to take a spot in whatever session they have available.

Sam has been attending Stagedoor as a camper for four years, and it is the perfect place for him. He learns new acting, dancing, and singing skills from highly regarded theatre professionals, and also gets the taste of independence that I wanted him to have each summer. Every year, he grows as an actor and a person, and I am grateful that we are able to send him there.

There are several other fantastic options out there for overnight theatre summer camps, and I encourage you to research what fits best with your child's geographical, monetary, and emotional needs.

There are also several workshop-style camps offered by the Broadway community within New York City itself. These camps will often send out representatives to local towns to audition students, or students can send in audition videotapes. The camps are usually held in studios within the city, so out of state students should prepare to stay for a week or two in a hotel or try to rent out an apartment (try www.vrbo.com or AirB&B.) Being that it is New York, hotels will often offer discounts for long-term stays. We have had several friends attend NYC workshop camps and what they love about them is that they get lots of feedback from agents and casting directors. Some camps offer classes and workshops with current and past Broadway stars. A few even include field trips to see Broadway shows with your child's camp tuition. (Although there are several out there, we have had friends who enjoy Broadway Arts Advantage (BAA), Open Jar, and the Stella Adler Studio.) In addition, theatrical universities around New York will offer summer camp options, including Pace University.

We have also had friends do similar special workshop-style camps in Los Angeles. Because it is L.A., there are several on-camera camps that will include visits from stars of television and film or well-known casting directors or agents. There are also some really unique summertime opportunities: The Groundlings, a comedy and improv theatre, holds summer classes for teens to hone stand-up skills, and UCLA offers student housing along with its wide variety of week-long acting camps.

My home state of Michigan is home to the famous Interlochen Camp, which is also very well-loved by acting, dancing, and singing kids who want to go to overnight camp. They also add the focus of playing musical instruments, which adds an extra appeal for prospective campers.

There are also wonderful local theatre day-camps in every city. Usually sponsored by community theaters and acting studios, these camps are tailored to different ages and sometimes offer a wide variety of training (i.e. Shakespeare, musical theatre, on-camera acting.) They are also often thematic camps that focus on one particular show per session. In Arizona, one local theatre offered "Wicked" camp, where the kids get to do scenes from the Broadway musical "Wicked." My favorite day camps are the ones where the kids write their own play, based on a book or a scene from a television show or movie. Sam did "Diary of a Wimpy Kid Camp" one summer, and the kids wrote their own play based on chapters from the book (this was before the movie versions came out.) I think learning how to write, direct, and produce a show are just as important as acting in one.

The bottom line is this: acting is a skill that requires year-round practice. Summer is a great time to focus on learning new techniques and honing the skills you have learned throughout the year. Take advantage of the extra time in your child's day now that school is out to have some fun and try new things!

E. Instruments: Children who love to sing and dance also really enjoy playing a musical instrument. Playing an instrument helps with learning melodies and harmonies for singing and understanding rhythm for dancing. Many child actors also dream of writing and composing their own music for shows one day. Studies have shown that the earlier children start learning how to play an instrument, the more success they will have in keeping that skill as they become adults.

Most public schools offer free band programs during the school day for children to learn to play a wide variety of instruments. There are also separate programs for strings, woodwinds, and percussion instruments. Learning any of these instruments will be extremely helpful for a career in stage acting.

Sam has been a part of shows that have required a knowledge of a certain musical instrument. He played the recorder in a professional production of "Gypsy" and played the saxophone in "The Princess and the Pea". Recently, one of Sam's peers had to quickly learn how to play the guitar for a show she in which she was cast. In "The Addams Family," the actor playing Uncle Fester has to learn to play the banjo for a pivotal scene. It is never too late to pick up a musical instrument and learn to play. However, the earlier you are able to read sheet music for one instrument the easier it will be to learn how to play another instrument.

F. Special Skills: When you are looking for an agent or submitting your child for an audition, there will often be a section inquiring whether your child has any special skills. This can include anything from gymnastic or tumbling skills, to puppeteering or even water-skiing. We receive several casting notices a day that will include a line that will say "Skateboarding skills a plus" or "Need to be convincing as a basketball/ baseball/football player."

The Broadway revival of "Pippin" looks more like a circus than a traditional musical, and a majority of the ensemble are actual Cirque De Soleil performers. The Broadway production of "Bring It On" and its subsequent tour was cast mostly with professional or college cheerleaders. Even roller skating is handy if you want to be part of a show like "Xanadu" or "Starlight Express."

We are also noticing more and more casting requests for children who speak fluent Spanish or French. Having a second language handy is very helpful for voice-over jobs or movies about an influential leader or sports figure (i.e., they are currently casting the movie "Pele" and the casting notices say that the boy auditioning for the role of "Young Pele" must be able to speak fluent Spanish.)

G. Dance Classes: If you have seen the musical production of "Billy Elliot," you know how increasingly important it is that aspiring male and female actors know how to dance. Broadway shows these days often require young actors to know how to be extremely proficient at jazz, tap, and ballet. Recent Broadway hits such as "Matilda" and Newsies" have some of the most elaborate dace numbers that have ever been staged. Being able to fake it for a scene or two may work for awhile, but, ultimately, you need to right skills to be able to be consistently cast in musicals.

Most dance studios offer weekly dance lessons in groups or teams that will perform in recitals or in competitions. With incredibly busy schedules that include auditions, voice lessons, acting classes, performances and school, finding time for young actors to add a weekly dance class can be almost impossible. More and more dance studios are realizing the need to allow students to schedule private dance lessons that are planned around the child's schedule. I encourage you to call your local dance studio to see what options are offered. We also have friends who have dance instructors who come to their home, but that can be difficult without having a good dance floor in your house.

We have found that the best time for Sam to brush up on his dance skills is during his time at overnight camp. Most acting camps offer a wide variety of dance classes and we always encourage him to choose one of these classes as part of his camp curriculum. Another great option is to do a master class with a visiting dance instructor at your local dance studio. Many dance studios, realizing the popularity of television reality shows like "So You Think You Can Dance" will hire well-known dancers to come into town to teach a workshop to aspiring young dancers.

Conclusion

The underlying message I would like to relay is that being a well-rounded child is very important for many reasons. As I stated, it certainly helps your child get cast in a variety of roles. More important, however, is that you want your child to realize that there is more to the world than show business. It would be great for them to have another activity that they enjoy if they decide to give it up acting.

CHAPTER FOUR: HEAD SHOTS

If you decide that you want to move forward with a potential career for your child, the first step is to get professional head shots of your child taken. And by professional, I mean a photographer who is trained to do head shots. Not someone who "thinks" they know what to do.

These pictures need to be taken by a photographer who is fully aware of what is required to take a good, quality professional headshot. There are specific things that the headshot must include and a photographer who specializes in wedding or portrait photography may not know how to properly frame the photograph.

Due to your child's changing face and "look," you will need to update your child's pictures quite frequently. When choosing your photographer, make sure you choose one who does not overcharge. Check around your area to see what the most reasonable rates in town are before selecting your photographer.

A. Three Types of Shots

Our photographer always likes to take 3 different shots to have in Sam's portfolio:

1. **Commercial:** This type of picture is for when you are submitting your child for television, movies or commercials. It has to be very animated: huge smile, excited facial expression, and the kind of friendly face you would want to watch on t.v.

Here is the most recent commercial headshot we had done of Sam: (Note the open-mouth smile. It took us some time to realize the importance of this detail. We thought it looked odd but it is actually very appealing to casting directors who want to see what your child looks like when they are full of enthusiasm. This can be hard to tell with a basic smile.)

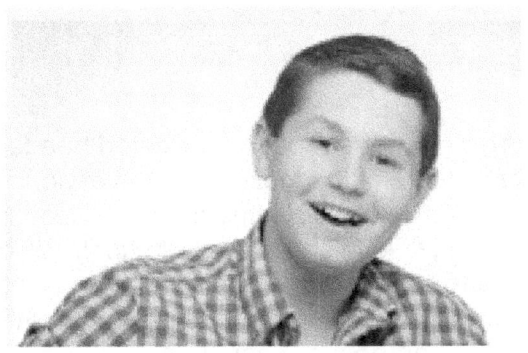

2. **Theatrical (classic)**: Think of the most recent Playbill you have browsed through at professional stage production. Theatrical head shots are the ones you will see in most playbills. This is the headshot you bring to auditions for Broadway, touring, or local professional theatrical productions. The goal of this shot is for the child to look like someone you would watch onstage. Also, it should show his versatility in his looks in that he would be believable in a variety of roles. This headshot should be easily used for an audition for "Tommy" one day and "The Sound of Music" the next.

Here is the most recent theatrical headshot we had done of Sam:

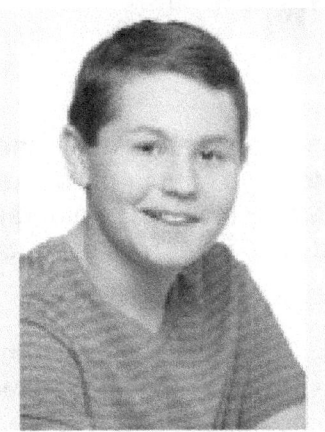

3. **Theatrical (Serious):** This is the most complicated headshot for many kids. This pose requires your child to look pensive, yet serious; thoughtful, yet incredibly deep. This style headshot is used in submissions for serious plays (ie "The Miracle Worker"), or for print modeling jobs. I also like to use this for a film or television role where the character description includes such words as "self confident" or "a leader." If done correctly, it can be the most effective headshot of the three.

Here is the most recent serious theatrical headshot we had done of Sam:

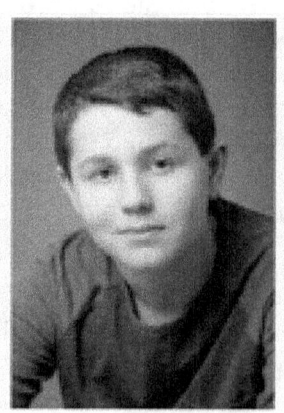

If you have an agent or are submitting to an agency, check to see what type of pictures they would like to have of your child. Additionally, agents often like to work with only a few specific local photographers whose work they are familiar with and already know the type of shots that your agent wants.

      B. Printing Head shots: There are not many printing companies that will print head shots exactly the way many agents would prefer, but there are several well-known companies in Los Angeles that will print it according to industry standards. They will ship to you in any location if you send them your headshot electronically. We have used these printing companies and the quality is great. I encourage you to Google "headshot printing Los Angeles" and read reviews before choosing a printing company. We have also used Costco or even Walgreens for quick headshot printing needs or for local auditions and they seem to do the trick as well!!

A final note: a good headshot is crucial for many reasons, but sometimes, your child can book a job directly from their headshot. The television show "The League" on FXX was looking to cast a flashback scene of their five male leads as pre-teens. I submitted Sam for the job and, because of his resemblance to the actor who plays Kevin, he was cast directly off of his headshot. We flew to L.A. that week, and he shot the scene. (You can see him on Episode 8 of Season 5. Smoking pot.)

CHAPTER FIVE: RESUME

Along with a good headshot, every child needs a resume to be able to start a profile with an agency or to submit for a role. Even if your child has no experience, you can include their age, height, weight and any special skills they have (ice skating champ, aerial dance star, etc.)

When creating your child's resume, keep in mind that you do not have to have just one version. I have a few handy that I can submit based on the job. We have one resume for theatrical auditions that includes all of Sam's voice training, theatre experience, and theatrical awards. For auditions that are for television and film, I use one that includes every televised appearance he has done (including news interviews) and the commercial work that he has done.

I do not like to include his age, as I think that it can be a distraction. Sam is 13 years old, but he is currently 5 foot 6 and about 120 pounds, making him appear about 14-15 years old. If I want to submit him for a role for a 14 year old on t.v., or for a teenage role in a play, putting his age on his resume might be a reason for casting directors to toss his resume aside without even reading it.

Whatever you do or do not include, remember that you are usually able to submit a cover letter if you are mailing or emailing a headshot and resume to the casting director. Instead of having a resume that is overcrowded with too many items, you can include any extra information that is pertinent to your child for that audition in the cover letter.

Whenever your child attends an audition, always have at least three copies of your child's headshot and resume, stapled back to back. If your headshot is not the same size as the resume, make sure you trim them to be the same size before you staple it. Many parents attend each audition with a briefcase or expandable folder with multiple headshot and resume copies ready to go. (I, on the other hand, usually arrive with these things crumpled at the bottom of my purse.)

Here is Sam's current resume. There are several styles to choose from out there, and different people swear by certain formats. (There are tons of books and online sources that will give you different options.) This has always been the format we have used, and it seems to work for us. Please remember that your resume should fit onto one page only.

SAM PRIMACK

National Tours:

The Addams Family Phoenix Entertainment   Pugsley Addams

Regional Theatre

The Sound of Music	Arizona Broadway Theatre	Frederich
A Christmas Story	Phoenix Theatre	Ralphie
The Color of Stars	Childsplay Theatre	Eddie
Gypsy	Phoenix Theatre	Clarence
Peter Pan	Valley Youth Theatre	Smee
The Laramie Project	Spotlight Youth Theatre	Various
How I Became A Pirate	Valley Youth Theatre	Jeremy
Charlotte's Web	Valley Youth Theatre	Wilbur
Dora the Explorer	Valley Youth Theatre	Boots
Nine	Phoenix Theatre	Young Guido
Winnie the Pooh	Valley Youth Theatre	Piglet
Pinkalicious	Valley Youth Theatre	Peter
Oliver	Greasepaint Youtheatre	Fagan's Boy
Snoopy!	Greasepaint Youtheatre	Woodstock
Tommy	Desert Stages Mainstage	Tommy,10
Peter Pan	Valley Youth Theatre	Tootles
The Hobbit	Valley Youth Theatre	Bofur

Awards:

National Youth Theatre: Best Actor 2103; Musical (Western Division)
National Youth Theatre: Best Actor 2012; Play (Western Division)
AriZoni Nomination: Best Supporting Actor in a Musical (Snoopy!)
National Youth Theatre Nomination: 2011 Best Actor (West Division)
VYT Stars Award: Best Actor in a Musical (Pinkalicious)

Training

Voice Lessons: Kelli James & Craig Bohmler
Stagedoor Manor: Summer Camp 2011, 2012, 2013

CHAPTER SIX:
THE AGENT

Whenever I tell people about Sam, the first question they usually ask is: "does he have an agent?"

I will begin with a little background to answer this question. The concept of my child needing an agent always made me uncomfortable. It always sounded so "E True Hollywood Story" and it wasn't something I ever heard of children having while I was growing up in Michigan. So, when someone suggested it to me, I laughed at the idea and never thought of it again until Sam told me he wanted one. He said that several of his theatre friends had agents, and they said it helped with getting more shows. So, we researched our local Arizona agencies and found one that people had great things to say about. We called and set up an interview. At this time, Sam was about 8 years old.

The agent told me to sit in the lobby and that she wanted to speak privately with Sam. She said she does this to make sure it is the child that wants the agent and not the parent. I thought it was a great idea and I sat and read magazines in the lobby and shielded my face in case I ran into any other moms I knew. I was embarrassed to be there.

About a half hour later, I heard a burst of hysterical laughter coming from the interview room. The agent emerged to tell me she had never had an interview with a child such as the one she had just had with Sam. Apparently, she asked him what he saw for himself in his future as an actor on television. He told her he would like to start with McDonalds commercials, then go to Disney shows and then launch a movie career. I'm sure he saw that on an "E True Hollywood Story" with me, but she was convinced that this was all his doing.

We signed a standard agent agreement that agreed to give the agent a portion of his earnings on all work that he books through the agent. This can vary from 10 to 20 percent, but the standard is 10 %.

The agent then had Sam come in to a different location that housed the agency's videotape equipment. There is a videographer on staff at the agency who creates a recording for the agency website. Any child that signs with the agency will be required to make a similar video. In it, the child states his name and age into a camera. He is then asked to tell a short story about anything he wanted (ie a favorite memory, story or trip). This is for the agency's digital file, and casting directors can go in there to get a sense of each actor after viewing their head shot. The digital file, along with the head shots, need to be updated quite frequently as your child ages.

Flash forward 5 years later and I have learned a lot since that time about the role of agents. I will divide this chapter into two segments: proceeding with an agent and proceeding without an agent.

SECTION ONE: PROCEEDING WITH AN AGENT

A. Local Agents

1. *Theatre:* In our home state of Arizona, you do not need an agent for local theatre. Theatre actors research, set up and attends auditions all on their own, or, if you are a child who doesn't drive, your parent does a lot of it! We have a few websites that advertise local theatre auditions: dates, times, ages needed and whether or not there will be any pay. These websites serve for both children and adult theaters. Our equity theaters have what they call "general auditions" or "generals" which are usually held in the summer prior to the next theatre season. For actors over age 16, you can often make an appointment for the general auditions. For shows that will be including some child actors, auditions are held in the fall or shortly before the show begins rehearsals. This is usually to make sure that the kids that are cast do not grow too much before rehearsals begin.

Sam's first professional theatre role was in a production of "Nine" at one of our professional equity theaters called Phoenix Theatre. He played the role of "Young Guido" for 5 weeks opposite a cast of very talented performers from New York and Arizona. (The New York-based actors are flown in and housed by the theatre and they are also provided per diem and a vehicle in addition to their salary) It was an amazing experience and he was given a nominal paycheck for his work. Not one of these actors needed an agent or used an agent to book these roles. The paychecks are set per equity rules and there is not much an agent can do. I found the audition notice online on one of our audition websites.

(I will note that Sam did do a production at Phoenix Theatre with a well-known Broadway actress who came in to do the production. This actress did have both an agent and a manager and from what I heard, by the time she paid both of them, she really didn't have much of a salary left over.)

2. *Commercials:* This is where the local agent comes in very handy. Generally, you do need a local agent to book an audition for a local print or commercial advertisement. This is because the agents receive the audition notices before anyone else, and your agent will pre-select which kids within their agency are potentially "right" for the role. The agent will set up the audition and notify you of your appointment time.

Now, as I said before, commercials are very appearance-based and this is just as true in local commercials as they are in national commercials. Also, the auditions are most often held during the school day because you are dealing with company executives who work business hours.

So, not only does your child need to be able to be available at any time during the day for auditions and callbacks for commercials, but you need to be available to drive them. It sounds funny to say it, but having a child interested in an acting/modeling career is actually a full-time job for their parents. This is especially true if you are located in a busy market for local commercial work.

3. *Film/Television Shows:* Los Angeles is an expensive place to live, and it turns out it is also an expensive place to film. So, more and more production companies are choosing to film t.v. and movies in states where they offer tax incentives to do so. Such cities as Portland, Detroit, and Albuquerque are offering huge tax incentives for local companies to film in their towns. So, if you are located in a city like that, a local agent will be used to hire actors for anywhere from extras to principal roles.

B. **Broadway or Touring Shows:**

When Sam was 10, he went online to check out the next season of our main Broadway touring theatre in Tempe, Arizona (The Gammage Theatre). We had been season ticket holders for many years, and we were excited to hear the lineup for the next year. He saw that "The Addams Family" was coming on it's first tour since ending its Broadway run. We had seen it on Broadway and really enjoyed it. So, he decided to do a little digging and see who was playing the role of the younger brother, Pugsley. What he found, instead, was an audition notice on several websites for the role. The auditions were going to be held in New York in two weeks.

Sam went into full force begging mode to see if he could go. He was in rehearsals for a professional local production and was only going to school for half-days since this theatre rehearsed during the day. The auditions fell during this show's "tech week" (see below for definition), and the theatre did not want him to miss a day of these important rehearsals. So, he did a little more digging and saw that they were accepting videotaped auditions. The casting company's website had a link to the song that they wanted him to sing and the "sides" they wanted him to read.

We went to his voice teacher, and together they recorded a video that had him singing the song (the producers requested it be the song "What If" from "The Addams Family" which is the main song Pugsley sings.) Then he read a scene involving Pugsley and Grandma Addams, and his voice teacher read Grandma's lines. We had a professional videographer do the video, simply because I did not know how to use an iPhone to videotape anything. (Since that time, I do a lot of the videotaping of auditions on my phone.)

Below is his audition video that we emailed to the casting director:

www.youtube.com/watch?v=sPygALH2Hrc

After we emailed it in, we went on about our lives until a week later when we received an email asking us to come to New York. They email informed us that Sam was in the finals for the role of Pugsley. We flew to New York and the producers whittled down the actors until it was only Sam and two other boys left. We left to go back to Arizona and about three weeks later, we received the call that he had been cast. (I wish I could tell you more about what all of this was like for me, but you will just have to wait for that book...needless to say, I was unprepared for any of it. The entire time, I thought our little journey to NYC would be a great story to tell my grandkids and I kept singing "I Hope I Get It" from Chorus Line to Sam because the whole thing was just so preposterous to me!)

None of this was done with an agent. While I did consider hiring one mid-process, here is why I did not: (and please note: Sam's Arizona agent could not be involved in any of this since it all took place in New York and was not part of her jurisdiction. So, she could neither help with any of my questions, nor could she earn any percentage of his tour salary)

1. This was a non-union (or non-equity) tour. Many agents in New York/LA will not represent actors in negotiations for non-union tours. I cannot speak for all agents, but I know that two of the actors on our tour were represented by the same New York agent, and that was her policy. That agency also did not like it when her actors went on tour, because that took them off the job market for a long period of time. Also, the salary is not high enough for an agent to take a percentage of and still allow the actor to have enough money to live on. But, I do know of New York agents who will be glad to help with non-union tours and to take money for doing so.

That being said, agents will often help your child make an appointment for an audition for a tour. Kids who have agents get to go ahead of the kids who arrive for an open call because they have an earlier audition time. However, there may be 30 kids with agents who are there at the same appointment "time" so they are seen in the order they arrive.

I don't believe that most agents would be upset if their client booked a non-union tour (in fact, several agents proudly advertise clients on their roster who are currently on tour on their agency websites). From what I have learned, many agencies would prefer their actors book a theatrical job that is local so that they are still able to audition for other roles during the day.

2. In a cool ironic twist, at the same time Sam was auditioning for Addams Family, his adult co-star in the professional Arizona production was auditioning for a role in the first national tour of the musical "Catch Me If You Can." They were both going back and forth to New York around the same time. This actor is a great friend and mentor to Sam, and he told us that oftentimes, producers prefer that the actor does not have an agent. It is easier on the production company, and makes it more personable than having to deal with a third party. So, we listened to our friend Scott and I'm so glad that we did. (And a shout out to Scott who is now on his second national tour with the company of "Memphis.")

48

3. *Entertainment Attorney:* What I did decide to do, however, was to consult an entertainment attorney in New York who dealt with contracts for actors on tour. She was able to review the legal documents and tell me what was standard as far as legal terms and conditions, and what we could negotiate. This, to me, was what I needed the most help with and was the one thing I couldn't do on my own (Event though I am an attorney, I have mainly specialized in Arizona criminal defense law and that was not very helpful in this situation!)

C. **New York/Los Angeles**: Here is where your child's dream of becoming "famous" can cause the most familial drama and financial drain. In a nutshell, what I have learned about getting an agent on either coast is the following: no agent will sign your child unless you move there. The reason is simple: they don't want to waste their time representing an actor who cannot be at an audition at a moment's notice.

While on tour, I contacted a very well-known New York based agency that specializes in child actors to see if we could talk about representation for Sam once the tour ended. The agent asked me one question: "Are you moving to New York?" When I said no, they said they couldn't meet with us. They told me to contact their Los Angeles office since it was closer to Phoenix. The Los Angeles office also would not meet with us unless we moved there.

We did meet with several LA agents when we came home from the tour, and they all asked the same question. When I pointed out that we could easily be in LA for an audition with a day's notice, some of them were intrigued. However, what I have learned this year is that the reality is that would mean we could be driving 6 hours (each way) to Los Angeles several times a week. We can fly there, but with 24 hours notice, the flights are still about $250 each way. With two of us going, that's almost $1,000 for a flight If money and time are not an issue for you, then this is not a problem. But with two other children at home, and a husband who works full time, to be able to leave the state at a moment's notice is very complicated for me.

While we were in the process of signing the Addams Family contract, we were contacted by a friend who noticed an audition for the role of Ralphie in the upcoming Broadway production of "A Christmas Story." Sam had recently played that role in a professional production at

Phoenix Theatre. The week of the audition, we were going to be in New York taking Sam to Stagedoor so it would be easy to go to an open call. We went, and Sam got a callback for the next day. Throughout the summer, he was asked to come back to six separate callbacks. Stagedoor Manor staff did transport him back and forth to the callbacks, but they charged us for the 4 hour daily journey and Sam didn't want to go to more than two callbacks because he didn't want to miss out on any more days at camp. At the end of the summer, once school began, he was asked to come back to New York for a final callback for the role of "Ralphie."

Each and every callback that summer started with one requirement: the kids had to be measured. If any child was 5 feet tall or over, they were immediately eliminated. (This is very common in Broadway and touring shows. 5 feet tall seems to be the height limit for many children's roles.) Sam made it through the height portion of all of the callbacks that summer. On the sixth trip to New York, he was officially 5 feet tall. So, he had taken six trips to New York City and we spent several thousand dollars in airfare, hotels, and drivers. It was an amazing experience for Sam to be a part of a Broadway audition. However, parents must understand that it is very costly. That is why agents want the child to live locally. No one wants a family to have to incur such expenses. (And please note: several rounds of callbacks are very typical for Broadway and/or touring shows. This is also very common in audition for movies and television.) Agents also want to know that if they are "pitching" one of their clients, that they will be at every callback and readily available for fittings or read-throughs.

(1) **What if you live "close" to Los Angeles or New York?** It is very tempting to tell an agency that you are financially able to commit to any and all out of state auditions if you reside within driving distance of a major market. However, it is not always as easy as it sounds. I have a friend who recently decided to try this out for herself and her 15 year old daughter, "Karen." She signed with a modeling agency in L.A. while still residing in Arizona. Her daughter was selected off of the agency's online headshot bank to come for an audition for a nationwide chain of stores. She drove the 12 hours for the first audition. She got a babysitter for her other children and spent the night at a hotel. A few days later, her daughter was asked to come back for a callback. This time they flew to and from California in the same day. Karen ultimately did not get the commercial, but keep in mind that had she done so, she would have had to go back to Los Angeles two more times: once for the fitting for the

outfits to be worn on the commercial and another time for the actual filming. None of these trips are paid for by the company or the agency. While Karen would have been paid well, the agency would still take 10% of her modeling paycheck. With taxes and the required Coogan Account payment (see below), it really would have been quite paltry. (On a side note, I found the exact same audition notice online through one of the online casting resources I like to consult. No agent was needed to go to the audition.)

(2) **Videotaped auditions:** While videotaped auditions are becoming very common, agents will still want your child to come to NY or LA very often so that they can be seen by casting directors in person. Some parents choose to tell an agent that they are in the process of moving to one of these cities in order to be able to get that agent to sign their child. However, this will all come crumbling down at one point for you if you do not actually move, or if you are unable to continue schlepping back and forth at a moment's notice to keep up the facade that you reside there.

I know of a family here in Arizona who decided to take their child out of high school for the year and signed with an agent under the guise that they were moving to Los Angeles. Both parents worked outside the home, although the father had more flexible hours than the mom. What this family learned was that there were many days where their son sat around waiting for a call to come to L.A. to audition. While he was enrolled in online school, his mother was dissatisfied with the education he was receiving online. Additionally, the child was extremely bored and lonely because all of his friends were attending school during the day and his parents were at work. The child, a theatre actor at heart, was not able to participate in local theatre productions because of the unpredictability of the last minute auditions.

This year, the family has chosen to put their son back into high school. They determined that there is plenty of time for him to live a life in Hollywood, but that high school years of homecoming dances, football games and yearbook clubs would never be available to him again.

(3) **Taking the plunge and moving**: Once the tour ended and we made our trip to Los Angeles to meet with agents, we also checked out the living situation. For us, it would not be so difficult to relocate part of our family. Arizona is only a drive away from LA, and my husband is done with work for the week as of Thursday afternoons. He

could come every Thursday for the weekend. We looked into schools for the younger kids and checked out rentals and housing prices.

While there, we visited Sam's friend "Steve" who had moved to L.A. at the age of 12 to pursue a career in t.v. and film. Steve is a very adorable boy, with bright blue eyes and blond hair. He and his mom rented a one bedroom apartment in a local beach town close to Los Angeles because of the high cost of living in the city. Steve slept in the living room on a blow-up bed and his mom had the bedroom. His dad would join them every weekend, taking the same flight from Phoenix to L.A. every Thursday night.

Steve and his mom had originally decided to register him for school online, to allow for flexibility in auditions. Almost every day, he went to an audition of some sort. His mom drove him and would wait in the lobby. He had a few commercial successes: guests shots on popular television shows and on well-known networks.   That summer, Steve had decided to take the high school equivalency exam so that he would be a high school graduate in the eyes of California law. Many child actors in California choose to do this so that they are more marketable to casting directors. The benefits for production companies are enormous. No on-set tutors are needed for the child, and the producers do not have to adhere to child labor laws to allow for schooling.

So, that summer, he was a 14 year old high school graduate with lots of time on his hands. Steve spent most of his days hanging out on the beach and waiting for the next audition or callback. The day before we left, Steve and his mom were notified by his agent that he had lost out on a major role in a television pilot. He was devastated because it was the closest he had come to his "big break." Steve had been to numerous auditions and callbacks for this show, and he had spent many hours dedicated to landing this role.

On the way home to Arizona, Sam turned to us and told us he that he was not ready for that kind of life. He said "I could move there and not get a job for years, or I could go home and audition for local shows that look fun to me and go to school with my friends." My husband and I let him be the one to decide this and none of us have any regrets over our choice. (Fearing the "E True Hollywood Story" where he blames his lack of success on us, I really wanted him to own this decision.)

Our feeling is that if Sam does get a job that requires us to move somewhere for a period of time, we would be happy to relocate. But, to move without any guarantee of work is a gamble he is not willing to take at this point in his life. The decision is something you as a family have to decide before you take the plunge and move to either coast.

It is certainly advantageous to live in New York or Los Angeles. Many Broadway shows begin with small "workshops" in the New York area where producers test out dialogue and musical numbers (this was portrayed very well in the t.v. show "Smash.") If your child is local and easily available to participate in workshops of shows that need children, it will only help them with casting director recognition if the show is ultimately produced on Broadway.

I will end this part with a quick story. Through our Arizona casting agency, Sam was cast in a "spec film" for a major motion picture that was to be shot in Arizona that summer. It was being directed by a well-known director and the scripts were all written and the sets were all built. The spec film was a way for the director to check out if the sets would look good on film and that the location was good for filming. While not providing a guarantee that Sam would be cast in the film, it provided him the opportunity to meet the director and to be able to set up an audition during the actual audition process. The producers on the set told me to plan to clear his schedule for the summer as he would most likely appear in the film in some way or another. He shot all day on various sets and was paid a nominal amount. We were told that we would receive the video shoot to add to our child's "reel." Well, we waited and waited. We never got the reel, and there were never any auditions set up. Turns out, the movie never got made. We don't know what happened and the casting company was never able to get us the reel.

Showbiz life is uncertain. Changing your life and your plans for a possibility is unfortunately part of the deal. Dealing with constant disappointment is a definite fact of this life.

4. **Commercial vs. Theatrical Agents**: If you do decide to move to either coast, you will see that actors there often have two different agents. One is the Commercial Agent and one is the Theatrical agent.

(a) **Commercial Agents:** Commercial agents focus only on commercials: both television and print. This agent wants you to be available at a moment's notice. The nature of the commercial business is very last-minute and it is important that you are prepared for an absolutely unpredictable life. The commercial agent that we met with in Los Angeles made it clear that we absolutely, 100%, had to live within the immediate audition area to sign with him and we had be always ready for a call.

(b) **Theatrical Agents**: The theatrical agent in Los Angeles actually focuses on television and film and not in theatre, as the term seems to imply.   Los Angeles is very focused on the film industry as they are the home to many network and film studios. New York theatrical agents do include theatre as part of the auditions that they book, but as I said before, certain agents will advise against any long tours as it takes that actor off the market for awhile. Broadway is a different story, as the salary is higher and the actor can still audition during the day.

I recently saw this advertisement placed by a L.A. based agency looking for new child talent. The words of this ad perfectly sum up the expectations that will be placed on you and your child:

New Client: happy, energetic fun and outspoken (5 years and older.) Parents must have a flexible schedule to take your child to auditions, on short notice, sometimes same day. Most auditions are M-F, some weekends. We are very strict about our talent getting to their auditions. No excuses, no exceptions. If your child is selected for representation, you must have a cell phone and internet access at all times.

5. **Manager:** Some actors have both an agent and a manager. What I have learned is that this seems to be beneficial for those actors who already have a well-established career. If your child does have this level of success, it may be necessary to have a manager. The way I see it at this point, is a manager is just another person we have to pay if Sam books a job. (They also take a percentage of the work booked.) However, this is one of those topics where everyone has a different opinion.

We met a family at Stagedoor who did use a manager for his children (all 3 were actors and 1 had just landed a role in "Annie" on

Broadway.) His rationale was that neither he nor his children were in this for the money. He wanted them to get as much exposure and as many opportunities as possible while they could. He felt having both an agent and a manager provided that for his children.

Conclusion to this section:

Whatever you decide to do as far as representation for your child, you must remember that no agent can guarantee success. Relocating your family for your child's career does not always guarantee success. Please keep this in your head and make sure your child understands this so that the expectations and pressures on everyone never exceed what is realistic.

If your child often auditions for local theatre or commercials in your hometown, you probably notice the same kids and parents over and over. This is true in New York and L.A as well. The same kids and moms show up to these auditions over and over, which helps them with recognition and staying on casting directors "radars." When you occasionally fly in and show up to an audition at Pearl Studios in New York (a common place for many auditions, as is Ripley-Grier Studios), you are an outsider in the community and it feels that way. Everyone knows each other (moms & kids) and they have all the scoop on every audition in town because they have been to all of them. It is not necessary to live in NY or LA to go the auditions, but it does put you at a disadvantage in many ways.

Also, relocation does not guarantee success. For every Elizabeth Berkely and Emma Stone, there are thousands of other kids wandering the beach all day with our friend "Steve," waiting for his big break while his childhood goes by.

SECTION TWO: PROCEEDING WITHOUT AN AGENT

So, the question remains: can your child make it "big" without having an agent in Los Angeles or New York and without you residing in another market that is producing large-scale films or television shows? I believe that the answer relies on several questions that you must ask yourself.

1. Money: How much money are you willing to spend: If I told you that you can find many of these auditions on a variety of websites, would you pay for the use of said websites? If your child is asked to come in person for an out of state audition, how much money are you willing to spend to get her there?

2. Time: How much time are you willing to give to this endeavor? Do you or your husband work full-time? Is your child involved in after-school activities that require them to be present frequently in order not to lose their spot? What about your other children? Do you have access to a computer at all times to submit your child to these websites to be considered for the role?

3. Help: If you were asked to bring your child in to an audition in New York or L.A. once they viewed your online submission, would you be able to leave your home and other children at a moment's notice? Do you have a good resource of help for your other children or pets?

A. Online Resources

Depending on your answers to section "E", I will let you know that there are, in fact, several online resources that you can use to submit your child for roles in everything from commercials to television shows to major motion pictures. Once you sign up for the casting service, each website will allow you to create a casting profile for your child. You can plug in everything from your child's resume to their special skills, head shots, and video reels. You can also select the locations in which you are willing to travel for an audition. The website will ask for the age range of roles you would like to be considered for and it is usually a pretty broad range (i.e. ages 9-12; ages 13-16, etc.)

These resources will also ask if you want to be considered for roles that do not pay, and also if you want to receive notices for student film auditions. This is up to you, but I like to keep all of my options open.

Once you are all set up, they will notify you as soon as any matches are found for auditions based on your criteria.

There are different costs associated with each website, so please look into each website before you decide what you are going to use.

Some will ask for either a yearly fee for unlimited submissions or you can do a pay as you go payment scale each time you submit. Some will allow unlimited videos to be posted as part of your child's profile and some charge a fee for each minute of video that is uploaded.

Usually, listings will say whether they will accept electronic submissions or if they require you to audition in person. Electronic submissions can mean anything from headshot and resume only, and some will ask that you submit your child's "reel." Many listings will even include a link to the "sides" that your child can read from the actual television show or film for a videotaped audition. Videotaped auditions can be done on your IPhone or you can have them done professionally. For auditions that are for large-scale networks or films, we go to our local on-camera acting studio and pay a fee for a professionally videotaped audition.

1. **Slate**: If you are making a videotaped audition, don't forget to have a "slate" at the beginning. This is where your child will hold up a sign with his name, age, and name of agency if they have one. You can also include the city and state where you reside, but I have stopped doing that as I don't want to point out the fact that we don't live in L.A.!

2. **Website Options**: There are many websites that you can use, including Actors Access, Backstage, Now Casting, and Children In Film. If I had to guess, I would say that I get about 5 to 10 audition notices per day. Keep in mind that if you have an agent, they also have access to these same casting websites, but they do get additional casting notices that the general public does not see.

I will end with a happy story about videotaped auditions. An Arizona friend named Amy Bender found a listing for an audition for a young girl for a major motion picture that was launching a nationwide talent search. She made a video of her daughter Landry reading some lines from a few plays and singing a few short songs. Landry was selected from submissions all over the country and she was ultimately cast in the movie "The Sitter" starring Jonah Hill. Following that film, she signed with Disney and was cast in a new television show on Disney XD called "Crash and Bernstein." Landry has a fabulous career ahead of her, all because her mom made a videotape.

Sometimes, magic can happen in your child's direction.

B. **Reality Shows:**

I know that many people love reality shows, especially ones that feature children. I really only enjoy watching "The Kardashians" because I can't seem to turn away (which also happens to me when I see someone being pulled over by police on the side of the road.) However, reality shows have become the place where performance careers are born.

There are two types of these shows that I have dubbed the "contest" reality show and the "reality" reality show. The "reality" reality shows are those that show you what goes on behind the scenes at places like child beauty pageants, cheerleading gyms, and pawn shops. The "contest" reality shows are the ones in which someone ultimately "wins" the show, such as Survivor, Amazing Race and America's Top Model.

In Arizona alone, we have seen several local actors "win" reality shows that have launched their careers. Phoenix actor Max Crumm made his Broadway debut as Danny in "Grease" after winning the role in the reality show "You're The One That I Want." Jordin Sparks did local theatre in Arizona before being crowned the "American Idol." Chelsea Kane moved to Los Angeles in high school after doing theatre, and while she landed a Disney contract, she really created a high profile by appearing on "Dancing With The Stars" and coming close to being the champion. As I stated above, Emma Stone was discovered through a reality show that was casting "The Next Partridge Family."

All of the young dancers on "Dance Moms" are now famous stars, touring the country and getting paid to teach dance workshops and sign autographs. I also happen to have a cousin who is on his own reality show for operating a pawn store, and it's been incredibly profitable. He's had dozens of paid television guest spots and has written a book.

Like it or not, reality shows have become the place to launch careers. Growing up in the 1980s, "Star Search" was pretty much all we had as far as televised talent shows. Now, there are shows everywhere from "America's Got Talent" to "The Voice" to "So You Think You Can Dance" that are giving us our next stars.

The advice that I have received from those in the know is to think twice before doing these shows, because they can really change your life. I guess that can be both good and bad. However, in the case of show business, even bad exposure is good exposure. It's actually pretty cool that kids from small towns can break into the business even if they don't have the financial means to relocate. A full-blown career can be launched in your own bedroom!

See also: Youtube videos, Vine, and self-made internet stars with songs they wrote themselves. (I know, now you are humming "Friday" to yourself. I apologize.) Sophia Grace & Rosie had their moms turn them into internet sensations at 5 years old by sending in homemade singing videos to Ellen DeGeneres. They don't even live in the United States and they have made it here as actresses and singers (on Disney Channel shows!) They are even authors! Those are some seriously smart stage moms!!

CHAPTER SEVEN: WORK PERMITS

Most states require your child have a work permit if they are going to be earning money doing a theatrical job. Each state is different, and when we went on tour, the production company was required to submit a permit for every single state in which we performed. This was a lot of paperwork for everyone and the parents also had to sign each and every permit!! One state even required that state social workers come check out the work environment of the children, even though we were there for just one night.

The states that are the most focused on the work permit are, of course, California and New York. Your child does not need to reside in these states to have a permit, but they do need to have one on file and up-to-date if they want to work there.

You can apply for the permits online, but allow plenty of time to fill out the forms and get them back into the state and approved. The State of California requires you to get signatures of your child's school confirming their enrollment and good status standing.

If you are meeting with agents, several will require that your child have work permits before they will even sign your child. It is a waste of time for them to sign your child if they cannot work right away.

When Sam got the day part on "The League," he did not have a California work permit (it was one of the only states we did not visit while on tour). You can apply for a temporary permit that will be good for 90 days while you wait for the official permit to come in. Of course, this comes with a fee, so it is good to be prepared in advance by having all your permits in order before your child lands a job.

If your child is cast in a tour, On Location Education (more on this company in the "Education" section) will get all the work permits throughout the country for you to sign. You do not need to get them on your own!

CHAPTER EIGHT: UNIONS

A. THEATRE: Equity vs. Non-Equity

There is nothing that incites more anger in the theatre community than the topic of equity vs. non-equity. Actor's equity is the union for working actors. It operates the same way that most unions do: it protects the rights of its workers by providing rules and regulations for employers to follow when hiring a union worker. For actors this includes limitations on the hours an actor can work per day and it provides for strict safety rules and regulations. Pension, health, and 401(K) benefits are provided by the Equity-League Pension, Healthy and 401(K) trust funds.

Equity shows are generally more expensive to produce, and they can only perform at equity venues throughout the country. So, more and more touring shows are becoming "non-union" tours This saves the production company lots of money. But, it puts a lot of Union actors out of work. In fact, Sam was not on the first National Tour of "The Addams Family." It was the second. The first tour was a Union (Equity) Tour, but it closed so that our Non-Union Tour could take over.

For child actors, it is generally not necessary to have an equity card to be a professional theatre actor. In fact, in most states, if your child has an equity card, they will no longer be able to perform at non-equity theaters. Once you have equity status, you are required by the Union to perform only at equity venues. This can be very limiting to actors that live in states that only have a few local equity theaters.

In order to earn equity status, you must perform at an equity venue and earn "points." (While equity actors are limited to performing at equity venues, the same is not true of non-equity actors. They can perform anywhere.) Sam has performed in enough local equity shows at this point that he could apply for his card. There is an application to fill out each time you perform at an equity theatre if you want to earn your points.

If you are a child actor in New York, having equity status will allow you to be seen before non-equity children at open calls. Also, it may enable you to make an appointment for an audition instead of attending the open call. I have seen New York casting notices that request to see equity only children. I have also seen casting notices from New York that specifically request to see non-equity children. Recently, I called a very well-known casting company in New York that was auditioning equity actors and were also casting a pre-teen boy. When I asked about the equity requirement, the casting director told me that they don't normally care if a child is equity or not, and that both non-equity and equity boys could attend the open call.

Some people have suggested getting Sam an "equity eligible" card which gets them to be able to be seen with other equity kids, but does not make them equity only actors. This seems like a good idea, and I will probably do that at some point.

B. FILM: Screen Actor's Guild (SAG)

Film and television actors also have a Union called the Screen Actor's Guild. This operates on a point system as well, although it works differently. The first time an actor performs in a SAG eligible television show or movie, they get their first "credit." At this time, they can choose whether or not to apply for their SAG card. The second SAG performance gives them their second "credit" and after this appearance, they must apply for their card. The SAG protects actors and provides for insurance in much the same way as the theatre union.

It is usually advantageous for an actor who is serious about work in television and film to have their SAG card. We receive many casting notices requesting SAG actors, and the ones that do not want SAG actors are usually looking to pay their actors as little as possible.

This topic will be discussed at length with you by a Los Angeles or New York based agent if you hire one, and they will want you to apply for your SAG card as soon as possible.

CHAPTER NINE: TOURS

This section will provide you with some general information about life for a child actor and his or her parent guardian while on a national tour. While every production company is different, I have found that a lot of my experience is pretty commonplace.

I will say, however, that not all touring companies are equal when it comes to pay or what they will and will not provide for you and your child in the contract. Many, if not the majority of tours are non-equity and the pay scale will vary amongst these touring companies. It is always worth it to ask for advice from other friends who have been on tour as to what they did or did not get as part of their compensation package. Agents may not always be helpful on this because many don't deal with non-union touring contracts. Please, please go through your contract with a fine-tooth comb before signing and make sure you understand what is and what is not covered. You can always ask for additional things in your contract, and the worst they can say is no. No one will take away a part from your child just for asking.

A. Casting Process: As I described above, the casting process can come in a wide array of experiences. Your child could be chosen to come in to audition from a videotaped audition. You could attend an open audition call (or two or three) in New York and get your callback that way. There are more and more "talent searches" being held by casting agents around the country, and your child could be discovered in this manner. Keep in mind, that whatever the method that lands your child in the final round of auditions, you could end up going back and forth to several auditions and callbacks. This is almost always on your dollar. No one is paying for your flights. The casting can take place immediately after final callbacks, or you could be forced to wait several months while the directors make sure they have the right adult actors before they cast the children. One thing is certain: it is a nail biting process and the ability to plan very far ahead is virtually impossible.

B. Rehearsals: The one thing that is certain is that rehearsals for a tour will take place in New York. And, the actors are expected to provide and pay for their own housing during rehearsals. Let me repeat this: you must have your own housing during the 2-4 weeks of rehearsals. This is because, if you are an actor, you are supposed to live in New York!! (I have only heard of one exception to this rule and this was

66

negotiated by the company with the young actor's parents in advance. The trade-off was that the tour would not pay for the actor to have a tutor on tour and required that the child be homeschooled at the parent's expense.)

Our family stayed at a hotel during the 3 week rehearsal process. It was not cheap, and the only payment we received during that time was per diem for Sam and I (Per diem means a weekly cash allowance for food.) I actually didn't fully understand this part of the deal and the producers were wonderful in helping me figure out where to live.

Our other Pugsley lived outside of New York in a suburb of New Jersey. He was able to go back and forth to his house each night during rehearsals. It was, however, an hour each way, which meant that his parent/guardian had to stay in the city during the entire school and rehearsal time each day-up to 8 hours a day. I will never forget seeing his dad going to multiple movies in the same day just to have something to do! The benefit of living in a hotel in Chelsea was that I could drop off Sam and go back home to the hotel.

Once the show moves out of New York and into the venue in which the technical rehearsals begin, the production company will begin paying for your housing (ie hotels that they choose for the cast) and your child will start receiving their weekly tour salary.

a. *School*: If your child is cast in a touring show, the production company will generally provide you with a tutor during the rehearsal period and on the road. This is not something you pay for. It is provided for you by the production company. This is also true of Broadway shows and television shows and movies. Please read the next chapter "Education," for all of the schooling details and information.

*Note: the production company will provide transportation for you and your child to fly home from the tour each time the show has a break and they will pay for your flight home at the end of the tour.

C. **Technical Rehearsals:** (or "tech week"): If your child has performed in theatre before, you know all about tech week. This is where the weeks of rehearsals are put to the test because all of the sound, lighting, props, costumes and makeup come together. There are very, very long hours and rehearsals in which the actors sit for hours without being utilized. Your child has to be present (and also has to do school.) It is a long, tiring week, but it is incredible to see your child perform on a professional venue for the first time. Seeing Sam up on the stage of the Schubert Theatre in New Haven, Connecticut where we held our tech week was one of the most amazing moments.

Important to note is that all of the staging, choreography and vocal training for the show is done during the rehearsal process. Once it is all complete, the choreographer and vocal trainer used for the show will not travel with the tour. Usually, a cast member is designed the "dance captain" during the run of the show, and any changes that need to be made along the way are handled by that actor.

D. Luggage: Our production company told us that we were allowed to bring two suitcases per person. We had to be very strategic in what to pack because there were weeks where we would be in a cold climate one day, and on the beach the next day. All the luggage would travel with us, and each actor could bring a backpack or small bag with them on the bus or plane.

The boys were also allowed to bring one suitcase with all of their school books and school supplies. This suitcase would travel with us to each location on the crew trucks, and be loaded straight into the theatre so the boys could immediately start school at each location.

E. Bus & Trucks vs Flights: Most tours operate with a combination of both bus and airplane travel. The term "bus and truck" means that the cast is transported for most of the tour via bus, and the set and props go on large trucks. We did mostly travel on a Greyhound-style bus, but we did take several flights to get us to locations that required a longer than average bus trip.

One of the differences between union and non-union tours is the fact that Union shows limit the number of hours that their cast can legally be on the bus per day. We didn't have much of a time limit, and we did have 12-15 hour bus days.

Our bus broke down a few times, and rain leaked onto the luggage below. It happens, and we just had to deal with the inconveniences.

F. Hotels: From what I have learned, the housing situation can be taken care of one of two ways and it usually depends on the production company as to what is done.

1. The production company chooses the hotel for each city: The entire period of time in which you are on the road, you will be housed in a hotel that the company has booked in advance. There is no planning, no stress on the actors, and we were usually all housed on the same floor. The hotels were (generally) very reliable chain hotels that were clean and some of them had extra bonuses like pools and gyms.

Some hotels had free continental breakfasts and happy hours, and several had refrigerators in the rooms. We could also usually request a microwave if they didn't come standard with the room. Our hotel would most often be within walking distance of the theatre that we were performing in. If not, the production company would provide taxi or bus service for us to the venue.

One great advantage that I realized along the way was that every time we used a chain-style hotel, we could earn points for staying at that hotel through their loyalty program. I applied for the loyalty membership card at all of the major hotels and would add my number each time we checked in. (This is also true for the flights: Sam and I racked up lots of miles on our Southwest accounts and got some free flights out of the deal!)

Were there gross, disgusting hotels along the way? Absolutely. But this was usually in very, very small towns without a chain option. Nights like these made me realize that I needed a few necessities on the road: my own bedding, my own pillow, and my own towels. I decided this trumped my need for additional clothing!

2. The cast is given cash and they get to choose which hotel in each city: Again, this is up to the production company and people who have traveled this way seem to enjoy it. I have heard that for long "sit downs" (this is where you are in a city for a week or more playing the same venue), some cast members in this type of situation would all go in on a house rental in the city.

While I think this sounds like a great option, I really enjoyed the camaraderie that being in the same hotel provided our cast. We would gather at the hotel bar or restaurant before or after shows, and hang out in our pajamas in each other's rooms. It was a total throwback to college for me (but more on that in my "Momontour" book!)

G. Terminology:

Although Sam had been in several shows before the tour, there were still some new terms that I learned this time. A few of note included:

1. Company manager: Not to be confused with the stage manager, the company manager is the person who organizes daily life on the road. They are the business manager and your cruise ship director. The company manager is the person to whom we reported illnesses or personality problems with other cast members. The company manager's job is to maintain daily peace and harmony while making the show and travel run professionally each day.

2. Stage manager: The stage manager is the person who runs all the technical aspects of the show. They call "places" for the actors, give notes on what went wrong and right in each performance, run the sound and lighting cues, and make sure the show itself goes smoothly each and every time.

3. Crew: There are many, many crew members. There are the crew members who load and unload the set into each city and venue. There are the "behind the scenes" crew members such as the makeup artist, the costumer, and the prop manager. Crew members generally travel on a different bus from the cast as they need to arrive ahead of everyone else to set up all of these elements.

4. Band: Depending on your show, you can have a large band that travels with your show, or you can have a smaller band comprised of local musicians that are familiar with your music when you arrive. You can also have a combination of both. Whatever you have, you will aways have a Band Leader and a few musicians who will travel with the tour. The band leader also helps the actors vocally warm up before every show and will adjust notes or keys depending on their vocal needs.

5. Understudy and Swing: The Addams Family is a unique show in that there are certain body-types that are needed to play a role. Lurch has to be very tall, and Uncle Fester needs to be short and stout.

So, each and every main character had an understudy with a similar body type in the cast. The understudies also played the ensemble roles of "The Addams Family Ancestors."

But, if the cast loses one of the ensemble members to perform their Understudy role that show, it will throw off the choreography. This is where a swing cast member comes into play. They can usually take over for several actors if one piece of the puzzle is missing. We did not have any swing cast members, so if there was a casting change for a show, the ensemble members had to re-stage the choreography for that day. This is where our dance captain's job usually kicked into high-gear.

6. Merchandise: Often referred to as the "merch," our tour had a traveling retail shop that would set up at every theatre we went to that included Addams Family t-shirts, water bottles and keychains. The merchandise operator traveled on our bus with us, and that was nice because she was another adult that was not involved in the stage show. She was often able to have meals and go on field trips with Sam and I.

7. "Talk-Back": Every once in a while, there will be an opportunity for audience members to stay after the show ends to sit and ask cast members anything they want about being in a show. This usually happens once a week for Broadway shows, and it usually happened for us in cities where we were in town for more than a few days. The cast does not have to participate, so we had a sign-up sheet backstage to see which cast members were interested in being part of the talk-back.

H. A Day In The Life on Tour

I will now walk you through what a day in the life of a multi-city, bus and truck tour is like. For purposes of being able to include as many details as possible, I will use a hypothetical example of a travel day in which we leave Dayton, Ohio and head to Detroit, MI.

1. *City sheet*: A few days before we arrived in a new city, our company manager would pass out "city sheets." This sheet would tell us a little history about the city that we were going to, including its most famous residents and sightseeing suggestions. It would then give us information about our hotel, including whether or not there were going to

71

be any extra amenities. It would also include information on local gyms and grocery stores, and which restaurants were open late. We would also get the information on the proximity of the theatre to the hotel, and how we would be transported to and from the theatre. This was a great tool in planning how we were going to spend our time, especially if we were there for more than a day or so.

In our hypothetical example, our Detroit city sheet tells us about the Motown Museum and the Renaissance Center, as well as the fact that our hotel serves a free breakfast. The sheet tells us that the restaurant adjoining our hotel will stay open late for the cast. It advises us that the gym down the street will let cast members drop in as guests for $5 a day, and that the theatre is a ten minute drive from the hotel. It will advise us what time we need to be in the hotel lobby if we will be using the transportation provided by the company. (Some cast members choose to rent a car to explore the city on their own, and oftentimes cast members have family or friends residing in the city who will drive them around town.)

2. *Bus call time*: Our city sheet tells us that we will be leaving for Detroit at 6:00 a.m., so our luggage needs to be loaded onto the bus by 5:50 a.m. The cast and crew must physically be in the bus by 5:55 a.m. Early bus call days were best planned by having our luggage completely packed up the evening prior. We would also make sure to receive both a hotel wake-up call and to have an alarm set in our room or on our phone. The bus will be located outside the hotel and to the right, near the entrance but away from the front door.

Knowing that I am not good early in the morning, I would usually sleep in whatever clothing I was going to wear on the bus that day. At the beginning of the tour, I would try to pick a cute pair of yoga pants or leggings, and a nice t-shirt or sweatshirt. About a month in, I wore my pajamas and slippers and stopped brushing my hair or applying any makeup. You completely lose all sense of vanity on tour, but the good thing is that everyone else does too!

3. *Luggage loaders:* I do not know if this is the norm, but our company designated two of our stronger male actors to be the bus luggage loaders. For a small amount of weekly extra pay, if we got our luggage down to the bus on time, the bus loaders would load and unload our luggage onto the bus so that we would not have to do the heavy lifting. It was great, and the luggage guys were especially great about

calling the actors if they were not down to the bus on time (and therefore helping you avoid oversleeping!)

4. *Bus seats*: Our tour company assigned everyone a bus seat on the very first day of the tour. The bus had two rows of two seats each, and everyone had to share a row with an assigned "bus buddy." What this meant was that one person would lay out and sleep on the two seats and one would sleep on the floor underneath. This was decided between the two actors in advance, and the floor sleeper would have floor "bedding" that they brought with them. The bus that we rode in rarely changed, so we kept all of our "bus linens" on the bus at all times.

Sam and I were "bus buddies" and he was a great floor sleeper.

There were a few exceptions to this rule: the first were the few actors who were able to negotiate their own bus rows in their contracts. This is something that probably comes with star status, or being very familiar with what to negotiate in a tour contract, but the same actors who had their own bus rows also got their own hotel rooms (everyone else had to choose a tour roommate during tech week. Of course, for me, that was Sam.)

The other exception was something called a "swing seat.": We had about 2-3 more bus seats available than the amount of cast members who rode on our bus. Each bus ride, our city sheet would let us know who got the "swing seat" on that bus ride. It happened on a continuing daily rotation, and even I got the swing seat several times!

5. *Quiet hours:* Our bus had designated quiet hours until 10 a.m. each day. This meant no loud voices so that everyone could go right back to sleep once they got on the bus. The bus was usually dead silent during those early hours on the bus.

6. *Bus stops*: There were three "Ps" that were not allowed on the bus: perfume, puking, and pooping. The perfume was easily controlled, the other two were not. The bus usually made stops every two hours at a rest stop or gas station (including during quiet hours), and there was always a lunch stop designated on our city sheet. But, if you needed to do either of the two "Ps" before a scheduled stop, you simply had to text our company manager and she would have the bus driver pull over as soon as possible. Being that the child actors and their guardians sat at the

back of the bus, we really appreciated not having to smell any additional bad smells!

a. *The Bus Crawl:* So, let's say it is still quiet hours and you need to get off the bus during one of the early morning stops. You are in the back of the bus, and everyone in the front is sleeping. They are sprawled across the rows, making it very difficult for you to get to the front without stepping on everyone. What to do? It's time to do the bus crawl. The bus crawl is an elaborate move in which you will walk on the arm rests all down the aisle, without ever touching the floor. We were taught the bus crawl at the very beginning of the tour, but grew more challenging as people accumulated more bus linens and the weather grew colder. It was very hard to do the bus crawl in boots!

7. *Bus fun:* What do you do on the bus for hours? Usually, the cast would watch iPads, read books, listen to music on headphones or sleep. There were a lot of crazy shenanigans that went on as well, but you will have to wait for the Momontour book for that!!

8. *Hotel check-in:* Once we arrived at our hotel, we would get off of the bus and grab our luggage. In our hypothetical situation, we are only going to be in Detroit for two nights. I only took one of my two giant suitcases off of the bus for that stop. Sam didn't take either of his suitcases off of the bus. I had consolidated all of the clothes and toiletries that Sam and I would need for those two nights. This was great for because it gave us more space in our hotel room, and made it much easier to load our luggage for our early bus call to Philadelphia a few days later.

Our company manager would check-in to the hotel for all of us, and would hand out keys to each set of roommates. We looked hilarious, standing in a line, half asleep with hair askew and wrinkled clothing, holding luggage waiting for our keys. Everyone would check in, and either go to their room to rest, or, if really motivated, would work out or take a walk around town.

9. *Company meeting:* In our hypothetical, we arrived in Detroit at 2:00 p.m. The show tonight is at 7:30 p.m. Normally, call time for actors is a half hour prior, at 7:00 p.m. But because this is a new venue, we must arrive for a company meeting at 5:30 p.m. The company meeting is very important. The cast would all sit inside the theatre, and the company manager would point out what was unique or different about the venue

that we were in that night. She would let us know where her office was located backstage, and where school was to be held for the boys inside the building. This was also the time for important company announcements, and to give important reminders about upcoming events.

The stage manager would then explain whether certain props or scenes would be cut or changed due to the size of the venue. Sometimes the venue was so small, we would not even be able to have our large velvet red curtain that so dramatically started our show. Either way, if cuts were to be made, the audience wouldn't notice. It was always a great show.

10. *Sound check:* Once the company meeting concluded, the cast would go onstage for a sound check. Each cast member sang a verse or two from their songs to make sure their portable microphones were working with that venue's sound system. Also, the band leader would check to make sure the instruments were tuned up and ready to go.

11. *Child understudy:* There were two Pugsleys, but only one needed at each performance. At the start of the tour, both boys were required to come to the half hour call time for every single show. The boys were also required to remain backstage at the theatre until a certain point in the show, in case the other Pugsley fell ill during the show. Once it was cleared for that boy to leave the theatre, we would usually go to dinner or go back to the hotel. However, after about a month, the producers just told us that if it was not our child's night to perform, we didn't have to sit backstage anymore. They just wanted us to only be about 10-15 minutes away in case of emergency.

12. *Performance schedule*: There was a schedule posted every two weeks that would list which boy would be performing on which day and time. If it was a "two show day," the listed boy would perform both shows. The production company was fabulous about letting the moms submit requests to have their son perform if it was in a town where they had family or friends. In my hypothetical, because we are in Detroit and it is my hometown, I have been granted my request to have Sam perform in 2 of the 3 shows we are doing here. In all of the time that we were on tour, there was only one day that both moms requested, and she and I resolved the conflict ahead of time on our own.

13. *Guardian duties*: "What in the world did you do all day?" Besides "how did it work with your other kids" and "what did they do for

school?" this was usually the number one question I was asked about my tour experience.

Well, the answer is complicated. To begin with, the guardians have a certain amount of required duties that are outlined by the company manager. The guardians must make sure the child goes to school. They must make sure the child is at their call time on time, and our company's rule was that we had to remain on the premises when our child is performing. We had to make sure our child gets on and off the tour bus at the correct time, and we hd to be in charge of their emotional, physical, and mental well-being at all times. This is, of course, because they are still kids, and you are still their mom. So, you are both your child's mom and his manager.

When your child is not needed at school or at a show, you are free to do whatever you want with them. But remember, there are no other kids to hang out with (besides the one who is probably performing right now,) so you are oftentimes their only friend. We did sometimes go on great field trips and adventures with the cast and they included us in their activities as much as possible. But while you can hang out with the cast and crew when they return from the show that night, you have remember that you are supposed to behave as a responsible adult.

Our production company allowed the moms on our tour the most amazing gift: the ability to switch out guardians when needed. We had different family members and friends fly out to various locations to be Sam's guardian so that I could go home. Sam got to bond with his father, both sets of grandparents, his aunt and uncle, and an incredible family friend who all flew out to various locations to take turns being his guardian. In turn, I got to be a part of my family and their life at home. Also, my other kids were able to frequently fly out and visit Sam in different parts of the country so that their bond stayed strong.

Being a guardian is exhausting, lonely and isolating. Most of the time, you are older than a lot of the cast members, and you cannot really relate to the daily reality of their lives. And, frankly, they can't really relate to your life. So, you figure out a way to make friends and to fit in. Again, I go into in depth how I handled this situation in my book, but make no mistake: it is very, very challenging. And it's incredibly rewarding. I was able to spend precious time with my son and create amazing, meaningful experiences around the country with him. I met some of the most fascinating and talented people I have ever met that I am happy I can call my friends. I wouldn't trade any of it for the world. Can you live your life according to this schedule and take care of a child actor? If the answer is no, that's totally fine. If the answer is yes, that's amazing. My answer was a bit of a combo, and I am still recovering a year later!

14. *Cast parties:* We had lots of incredible parties thrown by the production company at various locations: opening night parties, closing night parties, "someone is leaving the tour" parties, it's someone's birthday parties, etc etc. Certain cities also hosted after-parties for the cast, and these were usually attended by the season ticket holders and city luminaries. They were creative and fun and different in each location. We had dinner parties with "Addams Family"-themed food and drinks, and parties on the beach with volleyball and an open bar.

15. *"Papering the House"*: If we were arriving at a location for three or more days, we would often be given some free tickets to give out to local family and friends. This was usually because we would arrive on a Tuesday or Wednesday, and these nights were not as popular as the weekends. This was a great opportunity to fill up the house seats with local residents and create a good buzz around town about our show.

16. *Comp tickets*: Each cast member was also allowed to choose certain performances in which to get free tickets to give out to family or friends. The comps were limited by the amount of tickets sold in advance, but the production company was very generous with our requests as long as we filled out our request form ahead of time.

17. *Extra hotel rooms*: When my husband and kids were coming to visit, or when we had guardians coming in that wanted their own room, all we needed to do was to fill out a form with our company manager in advance and they would get their own hotel room at our company's discount rate.

18. *Golden Days:* Almost every single day of our six months on tour were either travel days, performance days, or both. But, every now and then, we would find ourselves with a "golden day." Usually occurring on a Monday during a week in which we were in one location for a long period of time, the golden day was a day where we had no travel and no performance. We were able to have time to sight-see and relax at our leisure. Sometimes, the company would even plan special activities for that day that included field trips or large meals.

19. *Days off:* There were a few actors on our tour who were faced with a dilemma: their best friend, aunt, uncle or cousin was getting married and they really wanted to attend. If they knew of this event before the tour began, they could request it and arrangements would be made to have their understudy fill in far in advance. There were sudden deaths and these were handled in the same manner. Did everyone get to go home for every birth, bar mitzvah or milestone? No. But that is true of almost any job in which you travel.

20. *After hours*: A typical day in the life of an actor on the road consists of an evening performance ending at around 10:30 p.m. , dinner at 11 p.m., then an excursion out to a party, bar or hangout. A late-night snack would occur around 2:00 a.m., then they would be off to bed or to some additional hotel hang-out time. Then they would wake up around noon, have breakfast, work-out, and lunch around 5:00 p.m.

21. *Laundry*: Almost every hotel that we went to had laundry machines on site. If not, there was a local laundromat nearby. I carried portable detergent and dryer sheets with me at all times, and made sure I had quarters ready to use in the machines. The problem was that everyone on the tour wanted to use the machines, so I found it easiest to do our laundry when the other actors had a show and Sam was not on that night.

21. *Lay-offs/Breaks:* Often throughout the course of a tour, there will be scheduled breaks (usually called lay-offs) for holidays or periods of time where there simply is no city booked. Our production company would offer the actors a choice: either you could choose to go home during the break (and your flights would be paid for by the company), or you could to go to another fun location for a few days that was sponsored by the company. The lay-offs included some days in New Orleans and some days in Atlanta. Both of these were cities in which we were not scheduled to perform, but were on the way to our next location. The company would pay for our flights and hotel, but either way, you would not be paid your salary during the lay-offs.

22. *Asia:* Our tour lasted for a total of 18 months. 6 months in the USA, 2 months in Asia, a month off, and then the remainder of the tour was back in the United States. We chose to negotiate in advance that Sam's contract would end after the first six months and that he would not to continue on to Asia. The main reason was that Asia was too far away

to be able to fly home or fly the other kids out and we decided that 6 months was a good amount of time for our family to be separated. For the other actors that went, it was an amazing experience. More and more tours are adding international legs to their schedules. There is a huge overseas market for American touring shows, especially in Asia and Canada. So, do not be surprised if, at some point, a tour that you are considering for your child adds an international segment to their schedule. If this is something that interests you, apply for a passport for your child as soon as possible in case they do book an international job.

23. *Packing for the road:* I found that there were several very helpful items to have handy while on tour. Here is a list of some of the things that I learned to bring with me along the way:

a. Travel luggage scale: If you are going to be on flights as part of your tour, you will need to make sure that you do not go over 50 pounds a bag for most airlines. Having this handy tool with you saves a lot of headaches at the airport.

b. Shower caddy: You have all seen them at Target or Walmart, and you probably used them at some point during college or camp. But shower caddies have another amazing usage while on tour: storage for your bus seat. You can attach a shower caddy to the window on your bus seat and put things such as headphones, books or snacks in them. Such a good idea, huh?

c. Water bottle: Think about how many bottles of water that you purchase while staying at a hotel. You don't really trust the cleanliness of the glasses and you are not sure if the sink water is going to poison you (ok, maybe this is just me!) But, if you bring a good, durable water bottle, you can fill up in the purified water machine in the hotel lobby as many times a day as you want. This is also great for long rehearsal hours because theaters can be incredibly dry. Bring one for you and one for your child actor (who will probably lose it a million times so write their name on it!)
**Coffee drinkers may also like to bring a good travel coffee mug for the same purpose! Many hotels have free coffee throughout the day.

d. Travel-sized Lysol and Febreeze: The hotel rooms just grossed me out after awhile and having these items handy was great. I would walk into our room and Lysol the bathrooms and t.v. remotes and Febreeze the sheets and towels.

  e. Towel wrap or robe: I'm not a big fan of the small hotel towels, and if you like to take your time getting ready after a nice shower, those small rags will not stay on very easily! I started out on the tour using "towel clips" to hold my towel on while blowing my hair, but realized that a towel wrap or travel robe made a lot more sense for me. Target has some great options in their college section.

  f. Candles/Glade spray: Yep. You need these. They make them in travel size. Just get them and you will thank me.

  g. Makeup remover or baby wipes: Be sure to have some of these in travel size at all times. Sam always had makeup all over his face from a show, and he didn't like spending too much time in his dressing room at the end of the night taking it off. This will save you lots of aggravation.

  h. Travel laundry bags: We each had our own and it made life a lot easier when it came time for laundry day. I also kept my dryer sheets and travel detergent in there.

  i. Humidifiers: Hotel rooms can be very, very dry. I found that my skin has never been so dry as it was during the six months living in hotels. So, some cast members used portable humidifiers. I had heard that many of these are not very effective, so pack lots of travel-sized lotions or stock up on the ones that they put in your hotel room.

  24. *Business Centers:* Nothing made me more excited when I checked into a hotel than seeing a full-blown business center in a hotel lobby. While you can do mostly everything via laptop computer these days, I really like to do a lot of my work on an actual computer. I'm also a very visual person so I loved being able to print out schedules, important emails, and plane reservations. Printers just make me very, very happy.

Conclusion:
  In conclusion, I can tell you that our family's journey on tour was incredible. We were lucky enough to have hired a live-in au pair who provided the daily consistency for our kids and our home. We had the additional finances to be able to allow me to take a leave of absence from

my job as a lawyer, and to be able to add flights and hotel rooms for our family whenever we needed to. We had a huge community of support from family and friends at home, and were afforded the flexibility from the producers of being able to switch out guardians.

Being a guardian is an extremely physical job. There were cold climates where we would have to carefully walk to the theatre or hotel on sidewalks filled with ice and snow. We would have to take our luggage up and down to our hotel rooms on our own. We would have to make sure our kids were rested, bathed, fed and while taking care of ourselves as well. With this many people in such close quarters living this type of life, daily illnesses were very common. The worst thing for a guardian was to be dealing with a sick child or being sick yourself. When deciding who is going to be your child's guardian, please take into account how very active a lifestyle this is, and do not put somebody in charge who is physically limited in any way.

There were also time changes from one state to the next, so your body has to quickly adjust to that as well. I had several days in which I had no idea what day it was, where we were, or what meal I was supposed to be on. I found it extremely exhausting at age 41, although the younger folks seemed to take it all in stride. But then again, I had to take care of more than just myself.

If there was a category of people called "Type A plus plus," that would be me. I planned every second of those 6 months down to the wire and most of the time I didn't get thrown if something changed. Flights get canceled, delayed, and the bus broke down more than once. We were snowed in at hotels in the middle of nowhere, and we would have to hop on a bus in bad weather to get to the next location on time. It was nerve wracking and exciting all at the same time.

Our guardians were flexible and we had lots and lots of help in case something did not go exactly as planned. I was very lucky in that I never missed a flight home for a birthday, recital, or graduation. I am very aware that I could have missed any number of milestones if something was changed or rescheduled.

No one can guarantee that any of this will work for you or your family in the same way, and you need to really think about all of the above before you commit to a tour.

CHAPTER TEN:
EDUCATION

A very controversial topic amongst parents of child actors is the topic of education. I encourage you to really read this section carefully. This is probably the most important part of what you will learn in this book and will help you decide if your child can handle this type of life.

A. On-Location

As I stated above, if your child is cast in a touring show or in a television show or movie, there will most likely be a tutor hired for your child. This is not a cost that you will have to incur as it is provided for by the production company. The main source of tutors for all child actors is a company called On-Location Education. On-Location educators are certified teachers who are used to teaching children who are only going to be with them for a short period of time. They are able to adapt to any other school district's curriculum and keep your child on track for when they return to their home schools.

In our situation, there were two Pugsleys on tour. Sam was in 6th grade and the other boy was in 5th grade. Per Arizona law, Sam had to be registered as a homeschool student if he was not going to be attending an Arizona school. However, our district helped provide us with resources for the 6th grade curriculum so that he would be learning the same thing as the kids at his school. There was one tutor assigned for both boys for the entire tour.

During the rehearsal period in New York, they attended "school" in the morning at the rehearsal studio. Our tutor would take turns teaching one child while the other child worked on their schoolwork or reading assignments It was very fair and equitable. In the afternoon, they would attend rehearsal at the same building. On-Location would require weekly reports on how many hours the student attended school and what subjects they were taught. The tutor was required to teach as many hours as the student's home district had for that year.

Sometimes during the rehearsal period, we would have extra school hours so that we could "bank" them for the days that we would be on the road for long periods of time, or days where the kids would be in long technical rehearsals. The character of Pugsley was on stage about 70 percent of the show, so there were days where their characters were not required for very many hours of rehearsal and we could bank school hours.

Once we hit the road, school hours and locations would change every day. If we were doing a 12 hour travel day, we would have school hours on the bus in the afternoon. The child actors, their guardians, and the tutor sat in the back of the bus so that the school did not disturb the adult actors. This required many things of a child: they had to be able to be in "school" and not be too loud. They had to be able to read and write on a bus, something that is difficult to do if you are prone to motion sickness. We were right next to the toilet, so people would always be coming and going and the kids had to be able to be focused and not distracted by the people around them. Difficult? Absolutely. Impossible? Not with the right child and the right teacher.

If we were in a city for more than a day, school would be held at the theatre, either in the dressing room or somewhere backstage. Each time we arrived at a new city, the boys would have to locate where school would be held, and the guardian would have to be able to accompany them to school each day.

School could also be held at the hotel where the cast was staying. We had school in conference rooms and even one day in the hotel lobby. The kids needed to be flexible and focused no matter where school was being held.

The most amazing thing about this type of schooling was the fact that sometimes our locations would provide lessons that the kids would only have ever read about in books. One day "school" was held at the Baseball Hall of Fame in upstate New York, and another day there was school at the Alamo in Texas. The production company would pay for these field trips and allow us chaperones to tag along. There were often afternoons where Sam was not in school and we would sightsee on our own. Every experience taught us something new about our country. These were incredible experiences that I wouldn't trade for anything.

The final message that I would like to convey is the following: being a child actor on tour during the school year is double the work of an adult actor. The child has to attend school all day, and perform at night. They come home at 10:30 or 11:00 at night, and have to be up and ready to go at 10:00 a.m. the next day. They also must study for exams and read required books. And while many child actors on tour are double cast

84

to give them a rest, they are still growing kids who need their quality rest and play. Both of these are put aside quite often during a tour.

B. On Set

Tutors are also provided for child actors who are on-set, no matter where the location or the amount of days. On-Location Education provides tutors on both coasts, and in any state. When Sam appeared as a day player on "The League", there were a total of 5 child actors on set. There was a tutor on the set provided by the production company for the day. We could utilize the teacher if we wanted to, but it was our spring break and so we chose not to.

The same as with being on tour, these kids do double the work of their adult peers on set. They must study their homework and their lines with the same amount of vigor in order to succeed. It is amazing to me that they have the focus and the stamina at such a young age!

*A note about the State of California: California has their own set of rules and regulations as far as on set tutoring. The teacher must be certified to teach in California, as opposed to the rest of the states that do not require the tutor to have local certification. On tours where there are performance stops in California, your tutor may be substituted for a few days for a local teacher.

C. Homeschool/Online School

A very popular alternative to traditional schooling is the homeschool option. This can be very beneficial for a child actor in many ways. They can be available for auditions at any time without having to miss school. They can rehearse late at night and not be concerned about having to get up early in the morning for school. When applying for work as an actor on a tour, if a child is schooled by their parent, it saves the production company the added cost of paying a tutor.

Our tutor had her own room at every hotel in every city, paid for the production company. They also had to pay for her plane ticket each time we flew to a city that was too far to reach by bus. If there is no tutor, this saves the company a lot of money.

When Sam's contract ended after six months, another Pugsley was hired. This boy was previously on a tour and his mom was his homeschool teacher. The same was true on our tour as well. This new Pugsley was a great commodity for a production company looking to save costs halfway through an 18 month tour. From what I hear, this is becoming very common on tours. I know that I could never teach Sam middle school math, and I know that I would probably bicker with Sam way too much to be an effective teacher for him. I am extremely grateful that I did not have to make that choice while on tour. Having him in school allowed me the free time that I needed to be able to live my own life and make sure that I was in good mental and physical health (I usually went to work out during school!) I would also use that time to make sure everything was running smoothly at home with my family.

Another popular option is in conjunction with homeschooling is online education. This can be done in addition to homeschooling for certain subjects or can include an entire curriculum. There are many options to choose from, and some are more costly than others. I know that the homeschooled Pugsley did use an online education service for certain subjects, but the challenge for him was being able to access the internet. Long travel days make it very difficult to get internet access for any significant period of time.

Recently, a friend's child was hired for a national tour of a well-known musical that has been touring for several years. The child role is usually played by a younger boy, around age 8. In her situation, her son is 11 years old but can easily pass for younger. After he was hired, the production company informed her that they would not be providing a tutor for the 4 boys performing in the tour. All of the boys would have to be homeschooled by their guardian. My friend was very concerned and was not prepared to school her son, who had been in an advanced school for several years and was taking accelerated math classes that two grades ahead of his own. She had to navigate how the homeschool system works, and how she could teach him advanced math when she herself didn't really remember a lot of it! She is currently on the road and learning as she goes.

A note about California: While performing at venues in California, the homeschooled Pugsley was required to utilize a local California teacher from On-Location. Again, this is because his mom was not certified to teach in the State. It was frustrating for he and his mom to have to start using a teacher for a short period of time. The teacher was required by the State to have him in school for the mandated hours per day, and he was not used to this type of situation. Again, your child must be completely flexible to be able to get through schooling on the road.

CHAPTER ELEVEN: FINANCES

A. Coogan Account

Jackie Coogan was a child actor on "The Little Rascals." According to published reports, his parents misappropriated his salary for their own use and he was left without any money as an adult. As a result, the "Coogan" law was enacted to protect child actors and to make sure that they have a savings account that they can access when they turn 18.

In certain states, a portion of your child's paycheck goes directly into this Coogan account. You are required to set up the account for your child, and only certain banks have the ability to maintain Coogan accounts. Not surprisingly, the main bank that does so, Actors Federal Credit Union, has offices in New York and California. If you do not reside in one of these states, you can apply for an account online.

What is interesting to me is the fact that this mandatory Coogan deduction is not required in every single state. So, when we were on tour, I had inquired as to whether or not we could just withhold the Coogan funds for performances that took place in those states. I was not trying to take away from Sam's salary, but as it got closer, I realized that we were going to need as much of his paycheck as possible to make this tour happen. As I described above, we flew out and switched out chaperones, and often paid for additional hotel rooms for our family when they came to visit. Sam knew from the first day that this was not going to result in a huge savings account for him, and that it was all about the experience and not the money.

That being said, we did end up putting funds into the Coogan account for the entire tour. It was extremely complicated to try to change his paycheck withholding each time we went into a new state. I'm glad we did, because that account will be there for him when he is older, and I know he will put it to good use.

B. Taxes

Another interesting topic that came up was the issue of filing taxes. Did Sam have to file a tax return in every single state he performed in? Our accountant said yes, although the majority of others said no. Ultimately, we only filed for Sam in our home state of Arizona. This is an issue you do need to address with your own accountant.

89

CHAPTER TWELVE: PRE-TEEN YEARS

Oh, the horror of the pre-teen years. We all look back on these years and shudder. Remember the acne, the braces, the strange hair appearing everywhere and the constant changing voice? Now, imagine if you are a pre-teen actor. Your appearance is the key to your career. Puberty is magnified to a degree most of us cannot even imagine.

I remember sitting with the producer on the first day of "Addams Family" rehearsal in New York, and I asked him, "What happens if the boys' voices start to change while they are on tour? Will they be replaced?" The producer smiled and told me that audiences are very forgiving when it comes to kids. He had told me not to worry. This was very reassuring to me, as I had already noticed tiny changes from when Sam first landed the role several months before.

Pugsley has a very beautiful song called "What If" that has some extremely high notes. (You can see Sam singing it on the audition video.) I will never forget the night about 5 months into the tour that his high note, which was so beautiful, suddenly sounded a little squeaky. I was sitting backstage with several cast members listening via speaker to Sam singing his song. (This is done for the entire show so that the actors know when to go onstage. Theaters often have speakers and television screens backstage so the actors can hear and watch what is going on onstage and make to sure that they don't miss their cues). When he sang his note and it suddenly squeaked, I immediately thought of Peter Brady and his "It's Time To Change" song. Every single cast member that was sitting backstage with me gave me a sad little smile. "The change" was starting for Sam.

The Pugsley that replaced Sam ended up doing the last 10 months of the tour. The young man was 13 when he started and turned 14 on the road. The band leader of the show had to lower the key of "What If" several times throughout this Pugsley's time on tour.

Throughout the 6 months that Sam was on tour, he grew five feet. He was 10 years old when he auditioned, 11 years old when he started rehearsals, and he turned 12 towards the end of the tour. Pugsley's outfits had to be altered very often, and certain props had to be adjusted to meet the changing sizes of both boys. (Pugsley is put up on a "torture chamber" and this prop is made to fit the actor's arms and legs.)

92

After Sam got home from the tour, we sat down and talked about what was next for him. He was very tall for a 12 year old boy. The casting notices for additional tours and Broadway shows for boys Sam's age would request a range of ages 9 to 12 years old. Sam was 5 foot 5 and looked more like a teenager than a boy. His voice was getting deeper every day. (A month after he got back from tour, he ended up in the finals for the role of Michael in the tour of "Elf." When he got to very last round of auditions, he physically towered over every other boy that was in the room. Michael, the boy in that show, was supposed to be around age 10.) We realized, sadly, that in the theatre world, he was no longer going to be able to play the little boy. Years of playing roles like "Young Guido" in "Nine'" ; "Young Tommy" in Tommy, etc. had come to an end.

It is a strange situation for a child to realize that the wonder and beauty of growth is also the reason for a portion of his life to end. He is happy that he is growing up, but sad that he cannot control the consequences of his growth. He was often sullen after we returned home, because he would wake up with a voice deeper than the day before, or pants that fit him yesterday were too short today.

This is when we decided to explore the on-screen world. Being a preteen boy is actually a hot commodity in that world, and we are still finding there is a lot out there. However, because of his height, Sam really fits better the 14-16 year old range in his appearance, instead of the 10-13 year old range. Too old to play 13, and too young to realistically play 16. It's a tough phase, but we are often reassured by friends that being tall will be very helpful as a stage actor as he gets older.

Sam has been on several auditions and callbacks for networks such as "Nickelodeon," but because we do not live in L.A., we are not able to go to every single audition that they hold. As with many auditions, if the casting directors and producers do not see you a lot, you can get lost in the shuffle. Remember: there are a lot of Sams out there who live in L.A., who are homeschooled or schooled online, who are able to go to every single audition. They are able to make the connections that sometimes make a huge difference in a casting situation.

Another problem is the fact that producers and casting directors would much rather hire an actor who is over 18 who could convincingly play a younger teenager. Not needing to provide on-set education, not having to adhere t child labor laws, and not having to accommodate an on-set guardian makes for a much easier situation for producers. It is hard to compete with the advantages a child actor can provide, even if you are a talented child actor. Unfortunately, there are a lot of 19 year olds who can easily pull off playing a 16 year old.

The best advice we have been given about these years is as follows: During your child's transition from child to teen actor, they still must train. Your child must continue to take classes and learn how to use their new voice and new body onstage. No matter what show you were in previously, or how famous you were, you are never too good to go back to community theatre or to play a part in a short film or local commercial. You will learn something in every experience that will help you as an actor.

We have really adhered to that theory with Sam. He has found a lot of great roles this past year in Arizona's community theatre that work for his age and size. We do not see this as him settling or giving up. In this past year, he stretched his comedy chops in a production of "The Princess and the Pea" as the Prince's right hand man and as "Smee" in "Peter Pan." He got to learn about portraying serious emotion in a production of "The Laramie Project." He also played Frederich in "The Sound of Music" in a local equity production (although by the end of the 2 month run, he was much taller than the adult actress playing Leisel!)

We are excited to see what he does next, no matter what challenges he will face along the way. Don't ever let your child give up if they are doing something they love!

CHAPTER THIRTEEN: COLLEGE

So, what happens once your budding actor finishes high school and is ready to head out into "the real world?" This is probably my favorite topic to discuss with older actors because I am always curious about the road that they took and what they would advise younger actors to do knowing what they know now. Being a lawyer, and a huge fan of arguing a topic in court two different ways, I will now present this issue and the pros and cons for both.

A. Go to College

There are some amazing collegiate programs for actors. The application processes are extremely competitive, requiring auditions for singing, dancing and acting. Admissions still look at grades, test scores, and extracurricular activities, so it is double the stress for anyone applying to an acting program. The very highly regarded colleges only have a few spots for students in the acting programs, and some require continued auditions throughout college to remain. (As an example, The University of Arizona will admit students for their Musical Theatre program as freshmen, but they still require an audition at the end of every school year for students to remain in the theatre program.) Some schools such as Pace University in New York will admit a student as a freshman in general theatre studies and will hold auditions for spots in their musical theatre program at the end of freshman year.

Pros: Going to college for theatre allows your child to learn and grow as an actor for four years, while being able to be a part of the college world. Your child will make great contacts and connections, and, as we know, a lot of the theatre world is about who you know. They will have a bachelor's degree and great college memories.

Cons: No college can teach your child to have a certain "look" or "sound." These programs may be able to help and fine tune what you already have, but they cannot teach talent. Your child will come out of college with a degree that is not really necessary to launch an acting career. An degree in theater may be helpful if your child ultimately decides to teach acting classes, but even then they may have to go back to school for a teaching degree. These kids will also emerge from college four years older, and may miss out on four years of great roles that they will never be right for again.

Also, several of the "Conservatory" schools are extremely expensive. Your child will graduate with a great degree, and a great deal of debt if you do not pay for it outright. Also, several of these schools do not teach general studies, so they are only learning music and drama for those 4 years. Additionally, some do not allow you to audition for shows outside of school, so you miss out on 4 years of resume-building experiences.

B. Skip College

The image of the "Star To Be" in "Annie," fresh off of the bus in New York City, is still a reality today. Several kids decide to head straight to L.A. or New York after high school and spend their days & nights waitressing or working in retail and going to auditions.

Pros: They are out there, at age 18 or 19, ready to work. They will have the flexibility to go to auditions and take classes at acting studios. They can do workshops and make important professional contacts. Your child will have an easier time getting an agent because they will be NY or LA residents.

Cons: What if they never get their big break? What if years go by and they are still working in retail, without a career or a plan? Is that a risk they are willing to take? Will they have the motivation and finances to go back to school if they decide to start graduate studies later in life?

As you can see, this is a topic that I don't really have the answer to. There are, however, a few other options out there that are great alternatives to the above choices.

C. Cruise Ships: If you have ever been on a cruise, one of the highlights is being able to see Broadway-style shows. The actors and productions are fantastic. One of the incredibly talented actresses on our "Addams Family" tour was an actress aboard Disney cruise ships for five years. She got to play every princess possible, perform in Disney-quality productions, and travel the world. The costumes and music were all top-notch, as were the connections that she made.

Performing on a cruise ship is becoming a very popular option for college-age actors. They get incredible acting experience during a time where they don't have family obligations to limit their travel opportunities.

They also get amazing life experience, and the jobs can last for years at a time.

   **Working at Disney world and Disneyland are also great options as well. Disney offers classes and also the opportunity to perform as a character or a performer at their parks. This looks great on a resume and is fantastic for making important connections.

D. College-non acting degree:

   Your child can still become an actor and go to college. They just don't necessarily need to major in theatre. A theatre-minded student can go get a four year degree in anything they want to, and still audition for community theatre in the city in which they are located.

   Your child can take nighttime or weekend theatre classes at their school and in their community. They will come out with a degree they can "fall back on" if acting doesn't work out, and you can feel good about the money that you spent on college.

E. Community college in New York or Los Angeles:

   Another great option is to have your child attend a local community college (or regular college), in or near New York City and Los Angeles. With a lighter load, your child can still audition as much as they want, and be in the city and be able to sign with an agent. The degree that they get is really not the issue, but being close to big auditions and still obtaining a college degree is a fantastic bonus.

*Note: Check out "AMDA" School in New York and Los Angeles (American Musical and Dramatic Academy.) This college provides a Bachelor in Fine Arts degree and great acting training (the NYC program is a 2 year program, and the L.A. program is a full 4 year program).

F. Summer Stock:

   Summer stock is a great addition to any actor's resume, and summer stock companies love to hire college-age actors hungry for experience. A lot of the summer stocks will also provide day jobs for the actors at their resorts or theaters, and hold rehearsals and performances at night. This is a fabulous experience for any actor and creates numerous professional connections. I encourage college kids to check out the online audition notices each spring.

G. Internships:

Companies always love having college-aged students who are willing to work for little or no money to do internships. Casting agencies, movie studios and equity theaters all offer fantastic internships for aspiring actors looking to learn part of the business and make contacts. In major markets such as Los Angeles, the majority of the theatre companies have an internship program in which theatre majors who are right out of college complete hours doing various jobs for the theatre (i.e. teaching voice classes to young students) and take classes from company members and get to perform in up to three productions in the season. They get to earn equity points and establish a relationship with a theatre and its company members. The internship culminates with a showcase at the end and several of the interns land paid jobs at the theatre once it ends.

Everything in this business is about making contacts and who you know and this is an incredible opportunity to do just that.

Conclusion:

I will end this chapter with the story of my friend Ben. We met Ben when he was in high school, and he was already a star in the local theatre scene. He was very handsome, had an amazing singing voice, and was a terrific actor. He had won several local theatre awards, and easily landed a spot in a very good musical theatre program in college. He graduated and headed to Los Angeles.

Ben has been in L.A. for a couple of years now. He works as a waiter during the day and auditions for theatrical and commercial productions as much as he can.   He pays his rent and his bills. He needs to continue to attend acting, dancing and singing workshops to keep up his skills, and these cost money. He does not have an agent, and although that is not a large barrier to getting auditions, he has been unable to find acting jobs that will pay the rent.

His parents have been helping him out financially as much as they can, but they had paid for him to attend four years of college already. Ben has friends doing the same thing as he is, but they are living with family in

L.A. in New York and not paying rent, or, they are living off of trust funds or inheritances.

Ben has recently decided that he wants to get his masters degree in musical theatre and drama studies, so that he can teach acting at a college level. Obtaining this degree will, of course, cost money, and will not guarantee a job in either acting or teaching.

There is no reason why Ben should not make it as an actor with his talent and charisma. But, that is just the reality of the business. Ben has several friends who are in similar situations. His very talented best friend just graduated from a very well-regarded east coast four-year acting conservatory, and is currently living back at home with his parents working retail and trying to pay off his student loans. He has another friend who moved to New York in high school because he landed a spot in next hot "boy band," and when nothing came of that, he stayed in New York and is currently working at a health club. Please think of these stories when deciding with your child what they want to do post high school.

CHAPTER FOURTEEN:

SMALL WORLD, BIG DREAMS, ONE CHILDHOOD

I am Jewish, and the Jewish community throughout the United States is incredibly small. There is a game that Jewish people play when they meet another Jewish person they have never met. It is jokingly called "Jewish Geography" and what it means is that if you sit down for about ten minutes, you can easily figure out someone you both know. Through summer camps, colleges, or familial relationships, it is a pretty easy game to play. I thought that we were the only community that could successfully play this game.

However, it turns out that the acting community is even smaller. Because of the fluid nature of acting, theatre actors have performed in venues all over the country. Community theatres, summer stock, and theatre schools, camps and classes connect this community in a way that really surprised me. It is a warm, supportive, incredible community. However, it's incredibly small.

My advice to you is to make sure that you and your child are ready to become a part of this community. If your child has behavioral problems or does not yet have the emotional skills to commit to this type of life, please wait. If you are unsure of how you would handle the pressure as a guardian, or how your family would cope with the changes, please wait. The community is small, and someone will remember a disaster child actor or parent, no matter how many years go by.

The most difficult part of showbiz life for us is the fact that it is very difficult to plan too far ahead. You never know when your child will get that next role and it becomes almost impossible to plan family vacations or purchase plane tickets to attend a family event. Life is constantly in limbo and we all walk around clinging our cellphones. Saying yes to a family trip may mean saying no to upcoming auditions or roles that you didn't even know existed when you planned the trip. We have had to cancel countless plane tickets, shuffle vacation dates, or find places for Sam to stay when he cannot leave down and we have got to go.

Also, when your child becomes a "star", you are giving them to the world. You are no longer the only one who gets to decide what is best for him. There are agents, managers, directors and producers who do that for you. I have not been able to get Sam a haircut for several years without having it approved by the costumer/makeup artist of the show he is currently in. I have to check with a variety of people to make sure it's ok each time a dentist or orthodontist wants to do something with his teeth. (Sam needed 6 teeth pulled at one point due to overcrowding, and to create the timing around his performances for such a thing was almost impossible.)

So much of what you decide to do with your child will depend on the rest of your family. There are tours that cast one child in a role, and another child as the understudy. The role is not considered "double-cast," which means that the only time the child understudy goes on is if the child cast in the role gets sick. I know several children who went on tour for months and only got to perform once or twice. There are kids who tour and never get to perform at all. Are you willing to change the life of your family for something like this? Some people say yes: it is a chance to tour the country and make great connections. Some who have done it say no: it was very frustrating for my child.

A lot of decisions can hinge on the moral and ethical principles of the family. So many roles for children can involve swearing and include discussions of topics considered inappropriate. Some adult actors around them may be partially clothed, or even nude in some scenes. This can happen on both the stage and screen. So many roles for pre-teen boys can include topics and language that may be too intense for many families.

I never really know what the right thing to do is. I am constantly questioning what decision is best, and I have a hard time figuring out who to ask. That is the reason I wrote this book. I hope I answered as many of your questions as possible. I don't claim to have all of the answers, and I'm still learning new things every day.

I would love for Sam to pursue his dreams and have a successful career in the art community as an adult. However, I am well aware of the reality of the life of an actor. Our tour had the most talented actors, dancers and singers that I have ever seen. Once the tour ended, many had to start from square one again. Several of the most talented actors I have ever seen are back working "regular jobs", auditioning and waiting for that next big break. A few of the actors on tour are newly married, and have made the decision for the sake of the relationship, they cannot go on tour again. A life devoted to acting is many things, but it is not family friendly. If your plans for the future include marriage and children, several career opportunities may have to be turned down, further limiting the jobs that may come along.

Conclusion:

No matter what the issue that will arise in your child's road to a career in acting, I think the answer will always be: are you really ready for this? Is your child really ready for this? Is your family able to handle it?

Your child has an entire lifetime to live out their dreams on the stage or screen, but the innocence and joy of youth goes by incredibly fast. How much of this time are you ready to give away? However, when will another opportunity come along in which you get to see the country or the world with your child and get paid for it as well?

I hope that this book has answered many of your questions and helped you decide what you want to do next. If you have any questions that I didn't answer, please visit www.momontour.com. Also, if you have anything additional to add to what I have written, please let me know. Things are always changing in this business, which is why it's great to have this book written electronically. I can always change or add new information depending on the current trends.

Whatever path you choose, I wish you and your family amazing success!!!

Allyson Ochs Primack

www.ingramcontent.com/pod-product-compliance
Lightning Source LLC
Chambersburg PA
CBHW071234170526
45165CB00003B/1091